British Railways
The First 25 Years

Volume 6
Central London
Southern Region

Farringdon

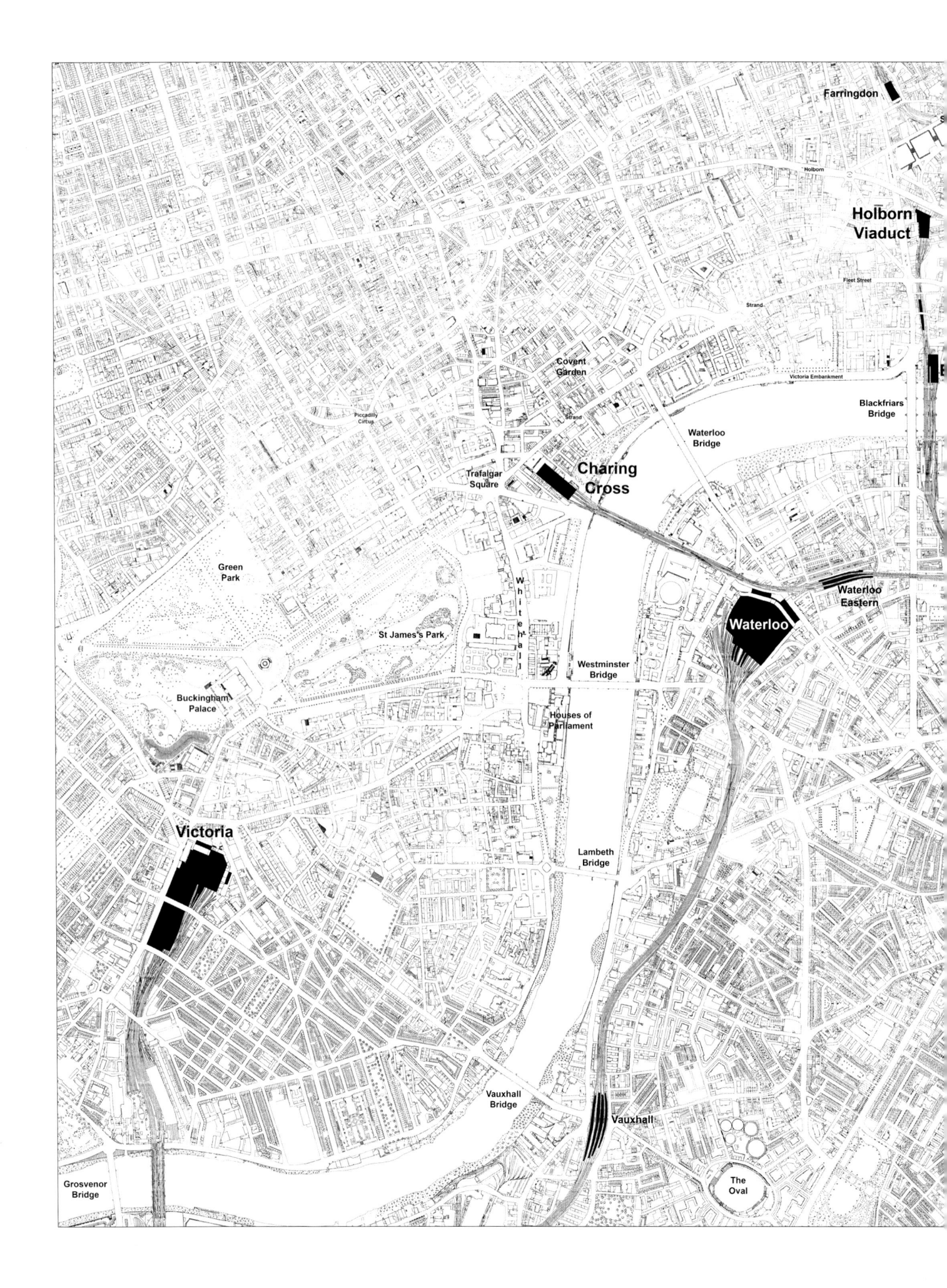

Holborn
Viaduct

Fleet Street

Strand

Covent
Garden

Victoria Embankment

Blackfriars
Bridge

Piccadilly
Circus

Strand

Waterloo
Bridge

Trafalgar
Square

Charing
Cross

Green
Park

Waterloo
Eastern

St James's Park

Whitehall

Waterloo

Westminster
Bridge

Buckingham
Palace

Houses of
Parliament

Victoria

Lambeth
Bridge

Vauxhall
Bridge

Vauxhall

Grosvenor
Bridge

The
Oval

BRITISH RAILWAYS
The First 25 Years

Volume 6 – Central London Southern Region

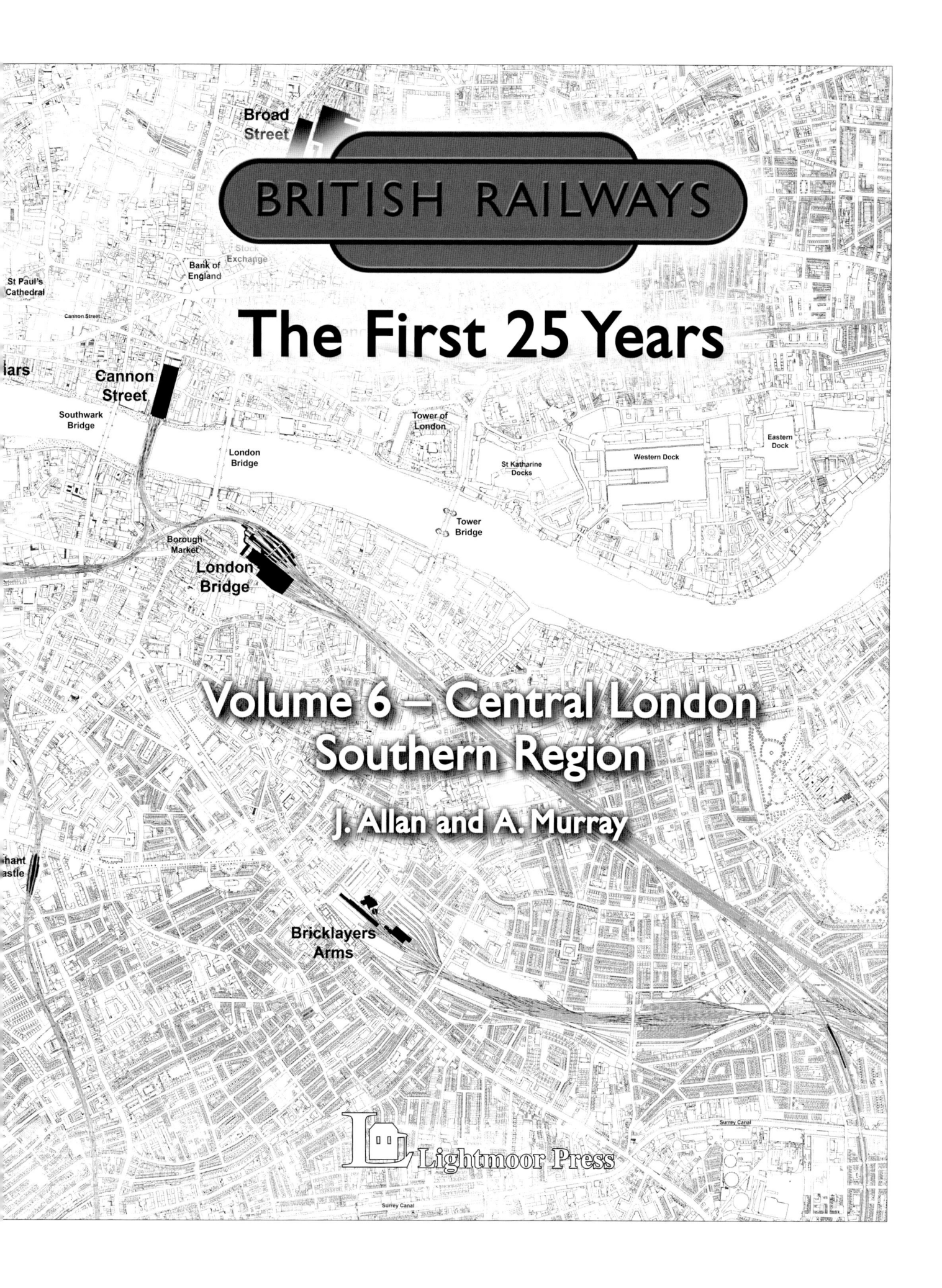

J. Allan and A. Murray

Lightmoor Press

Cover photographs

Front upper:
No. 4001 at London Bridge on 4th February 1954 was one of two four-car double-decker units introduced in November 1949 on the Charing Cross-Dartford line, in an experiment to increase the capacity of rush-hour services without lengthening trains or platforms. The Bulleid designed units packed 508 ordinary seats and 44 tip-up seats into each four-car set, compared to 386 seats in a standard '4-SUB'.

Front lower:
'Merchant Navy' No. 35028 *Clan Line* at Waterloo on a Bournemouth express alongside '4-COR' No. 3131. The 'Pacific' was preserved by the Merchant Navy Locomotive Preservation Society after purchase from British Railways at the end of Southern Region steam in July 1967.

Back upper:
Ex-SE&CR 'E' Class 4-4-0 No. 31166 on a parcels train at London Bridge in June 1953. It has no smokebox numberplate, and the No. 31166 has been painted on the buffer beam in Southern Railway style. It was allocated to Faversham at this date and spent much of the year in store, before it was transferred to Tonbridge in October 1953.

Back centre:
'Britannia' 4-6-2 No. 70004 *William Shakespeare* ready to depart from Victoria with the 'Golden Arrow'. After being displayed at the 1951 Festival of Britain, No. 70004 went to Stewarts Lane along with No. 70014 *Iron Duke* to work the 'Golden Arrow' and other Eastern section boat trains. It stayed there until June 1958 when it was transferred to the London Midland Region. The two lamp irons carrying the circular headcode discs were later raised by around eighteen inches on the two Southern Region 'Britannias'.

Back lower:
Electro-diesel (later Class '73') No. E6021 in front of the carriage shed spanning roads 7 to 11 at Clapham Junction in 1966. It was built in February of that year and delivered in blue with a small yellow warning panel. No. E6021 had a short working life because it sustained severe damage in a collision at East Croydon in January 1982 and was officially withdrawn three months later.

The Thames was crossed four times by Southern Region lines in the central London area. The line into Cannon Street was the furthest downstream. Until 1959, the station had a distinctive glass and cast iron roof over the train shed, but this was removed and all that remained were the supporting walls and the two towers. These were given Grade II listing in 1986 and are now part of the modern station, which was completely rebuilt in the late 20th Century.

© Lightmoor Press, J. Allan, A. Murray, 2017.
Designed by Stephen Phillips.

British Library Cataloguing-in-Publication Data.
A catalogue record for this book is available from the British Library.
ISBN 978-1-911038-29-0

All rights reserved. No part of this publication may be reproduced, stored in a retrieval system or transmitted in any form or by any means, electronic, mechanical, photocopying, recording or otherwise, without the written permission of the publisher.

LIGHTMOOR PRESS
Unit 144B, Lydney Trading Estate, Harbour Road,
Lydney, Gloucestershire GL15 4EJ
www.lightmoor.co.uk

Lightmoor Press is an imprint of
Black Dwarf Lightmoor Publications Ltd.

Printed in Poland
www.lfbookservices.co.uk

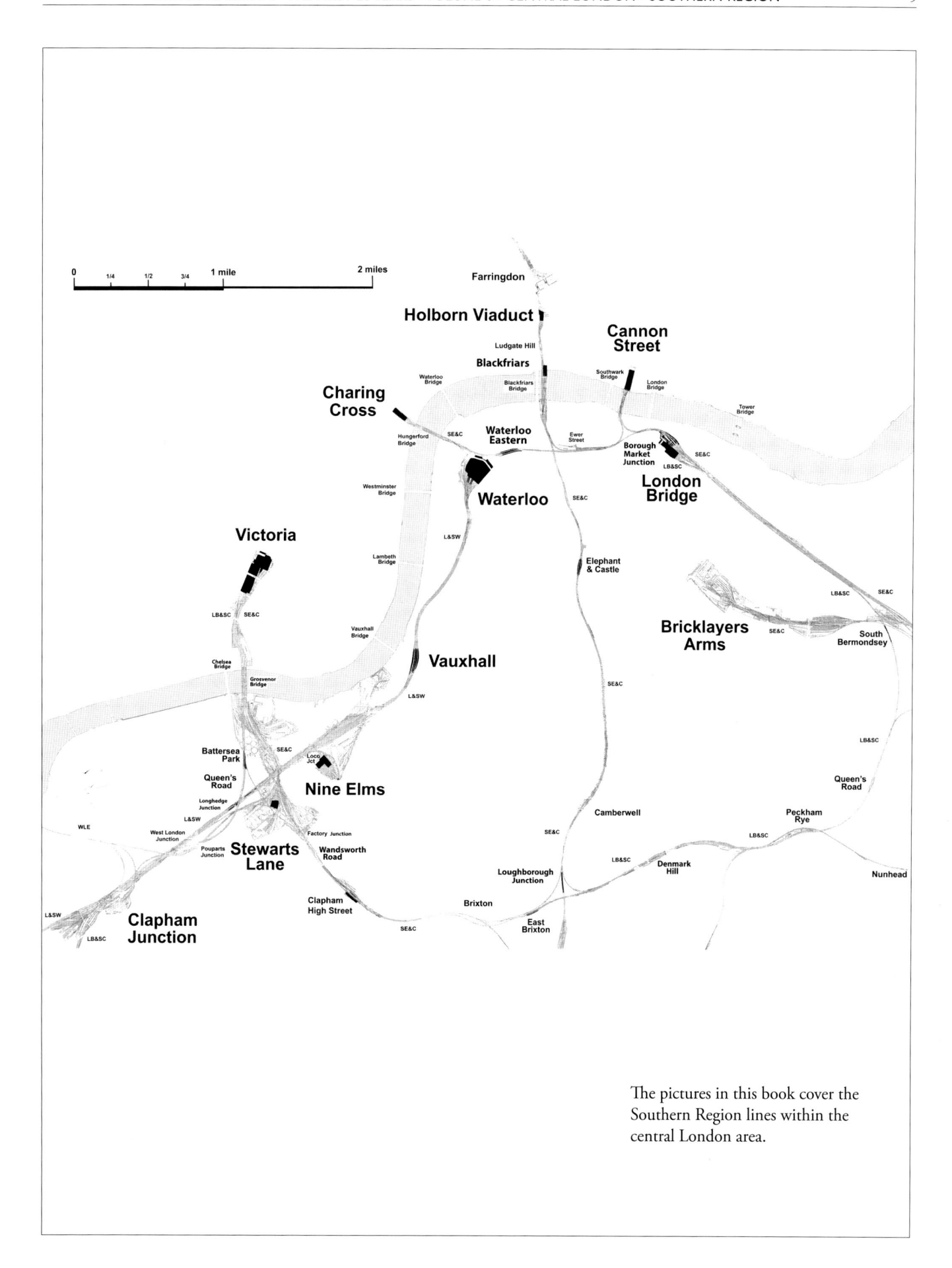

BRITISH RAILWAYS - THE FIRST 25 YEARS - VOLUME 6 - CENTRAL LONDON - SOUTHERN REGION

The pictures in this book cover the Southern Region lines within the central London area.

Contents

	Introduction and acknowledgements	7
1	**South Eastern & Chatham Railway stations**	**8**
	Ludgate Hill	9
	Blackfriars	10
	Holborn Viaduct	12
	Holborn Viaduct Low Level	16
	Charing Cross	18
	Waterloo Eastern	25
	Borough Market and Metropolitan Junctions	27
	Cannon Street	31
	London Bridge	39
2	**Bricklayers Arms**	**53**
	1950s	53
	1960s	56
3	**Holborn Viaduct to Loughborough Junction**	**59**
	Elephant & Castle	59
	Loughborough Junction	60
4	**South London Line**	**61**
	South Bermondsey	61
	Queen's Road Peckham	62
	Peckham Rye	63
	Wandsworth Road	64
	Battersea Park	65
5	**Victoria**	**66**
	1950s steam	68
	'Golden Arrow'	75
	'Night Ferry'	78
	Electric traction	80
6	**Victoria to Brixton**	**83**
	Battersea Park	84
	Stewarts Lane	85
	Clapham High Street	88
	Brixton	89
7	**Stewarts Lane**	**90**
	'Pacifics'	91
	4-4-0s	92
	Tank engines	95
	Diesels and electrics	99
8	**Waterloo**	**104**
	1950s steam	106
	Prototype diesels	110
	1960s steam	113
	Modern traction	127
9	**Vauxhall and Battersea L&SWR**	**130**
	Vauxhall	130
	Nine Elms	141
	Queen's Road Battersea	142
10	**Nine Elms**	**144**
	1950s	145
	1960s	150
	The end	159
11	**Clapham Junction**	**160**
	1950s	161
	Empty coaching stock (ECS) workings	173
	Cross-London freight	179
	1960s	182
	Diesels	193
	Electro-diesels	201
	EMUs in the 1960s and 1970s	204

Class 'M7' 0-4-4T No. 30123, viewed from the long footbridge connecting the two sides of the station and spanning the throat of the carriage sidings, busy on empty coaching stock pilot work at Clapham Junction in the 1950s. *The Lens of Sutton Association*

Introduction and Acknowledgements

This is the sixth in a series of books, depicting the first 25 years of British Railways, which will eventually cover the whole of the UK. We have been fortunate to have had access to hundreds of different pictures from which to choose the final selection presented here. At an early stage, we made the decision to include photographs spanning the early British Railways era through to the pre-TOPS diesels, although the emphasis is on that interesting transitional period of the late 1950s and early 1960s.

This volume covers the Southern Region lines in central London, from the terminus stations approximately to the edge of the area bounded by the South London Line, around only four miles out. We visit the three principal motive power depots serving the stations, Nine Elms, Stewarts Lane and Bricklayers Arms, before finishing with an extensive spotting session at Clapham Junction. This was the most complex and highest density network of lines in the country which, when viewed on a map, had the appearance of spaghetti, with routes criss-crossing each other as they fought for space on the way towards the capital.

No less than four pre-Grouping railways were responsible for the construction of this network, either building their own termini in the capital or sharing with one of the other companies. Two of them, the London, Chatham & Dover Railway (LC&DR) and the South Eastern Railway (SER), merged their operations in 1899 to form the South Eastern & Chatham Railway (SE&CR), although they remained separate legal entities. The other two, the London & South Western Railway (L&SWR) and the London, Brighton & South Coast Railway (LB&SCR) remained independent until all four companies were absorbed into the Southern Railway in the 1923 Grouping.

After Nationalisation in 1948, very little changed in the first decade, with a continuation of pre-1948 electric multiple units on the suburban services mixed with steam on freight and longer distance passenger trains, together with a handful of the early diesel-electric prototypes. The 1955 Modernisation Plan began a process of extending electrification, firstly on the Kent Coast lines and then in the late-1960s to the Bournemouth line from Waterloo which saw the final elimination of steam. The Southern Region had two very distinctive modern traction designs, the Birmingham Railway Carraige & Wagon Company (BR&CW) diesel-electric Type '3', which was developed specifically to meet its diesel requirements, and the electro-diesels which could operate on non-electrified lines as necessary. There was a slow evolution of the standard electric multiple unit but the 1960s designs were essentially little different from their predecessors, perpetuating slam-door suburban stock, and it was only in 1972 that the first prototypes with sliding doors appeared.

The mix of pictures in this book is constrained by the location and hence there is a preponderance of station and depot shots, but with, we hope, a good balance between the 'mundane' EMUs and the variety of steam, diesel and electric locomotives on the Region, plus a smattering of the glamorous named expresses which could be seen at Waterloo and Victoria. What is clear is that the Southern Region in the 1950s and 1960s was far from an all-EMU line.

Unlike earlier volumes, in recognition of the special nature of the area and to assist understanding, we have included detailed 1950s maps of the location of the principal stations and depots, showing how they fitted into the capital's streets and the way they inter-connected. Platform layouts are also provided for each of the termini.

Acknowledgements

We have had an immensely valuable contribution from Bob Waterman, who has provided much additional detail for the captions. Also, our thanks again go to Vic Smith for his help. Any errors remaining are of course entirely the responsibility of the authors.

The majority of the pictures in this volume are from the *www.Rail-Online.co.uk* collection. We have supplemented these with photographs from the *Lens of Sutton Association* collection. We have taken the opportunity to include many full page portraits which show the quality of some of these early photographs.

References

We have consulted a number of books to provide details of locomotives and workings. In particular, the RCTS BR Standard series, the Irwell Press *'Book of'* series, and *'The Allocation History of BR Diesels & Electrics'* have allowed us to include full details of allocations. Two books have been particularly helpful, *'Southern Electric 1909-1979'* by G.T. Moody and *'London's Termini'* by A.A. Jackson, as well as the Middleton Press line histories. We have also used the website *www.sixbellsjunction.co.uk* for information on railtours and special workings and *www.semgonline.com* for general information on headcodes and workings.

J. Allan and A. Murray 2017

The Southern Region only had one type of main line diesel locomotive in the first phase of British Railways' dieselisation. It was built to meet the Region's specific requirements and the whole class worked almost exclusively on the Southern until the early 1980s when they began to be used further afield. BRC&W Type '3' No. D6570 was in the carriage sidings at Clapham Junction in 1966. Built in September 1961, it became No. 33052 in 1974 and was withdrawn in 1997.

1 – South Eastern & Chatham Railway stations

An important influence in the development of the railways in London was that the companies on the south of the river were able to bring their lines right into the centre, property being cheaper than in the north of the city. A Royal Commission in 1846 had placed restrictions on railways entering the central area from the north side of the Thames. The southern companies took advantage of this and termini proliferated, with three lines crossing the Thames into the central area; one of them, the LC&DR, even built a link across the restricted area to the northern lines, mostly above ground and running in the shadow of St Paul's Cathedral. There were good economic reasons for this activity: unlike the northern companies they had a relatively small amount of goods and mineral traffic and therefore relied heavily on passenger traffic, for which access to the City of London and the West End was very important. Between 1860 and 1886, the stations which were to come under the ownership of the SE&CR were built, at Charing Cross, Cannon Street, Holborn Viaduct and St Pauls (later Blackfriars), joining London Bridge which dated back to 1836.

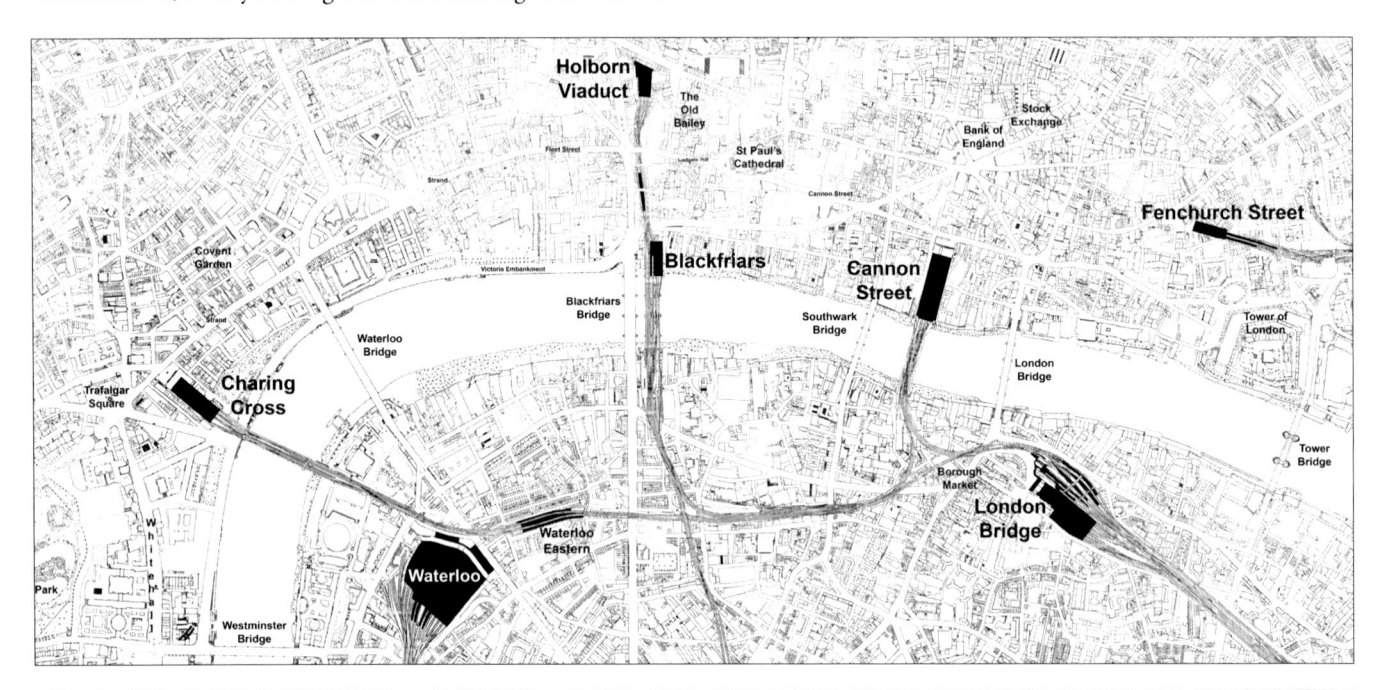

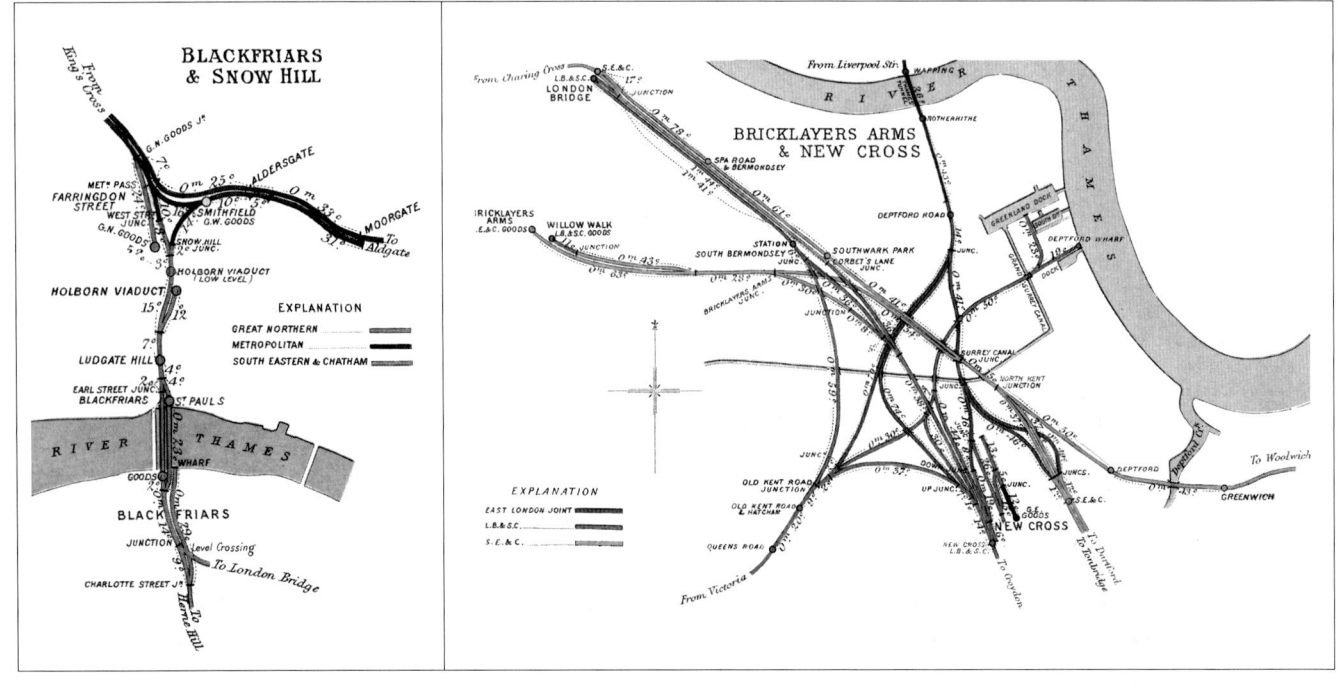

The RCH Junction diagrams illustrate the complexity of the ex-SE&CR lines around Holborn/Blackfriars, London Bridge and Bricklayers Arms.

Ludgate Hill

Until the end of the 20th Century, the LC&DR link to the Metropolitan Railway at Farringdon Street was the only direct route across the centre of London. Its sharp curves and steep gradients meant that it was used only for freight traffic from 1916 onwards, until it was modernised and re-opened for passenger traffic as part of the Thameslink project in 1988.

A temporary station at Ludgate Hill was opened in 1864 and a permanent one the following year. Although it was rebuilt in 1910, it was only 700 yards from Holborn Viaduct and became increasingly redundant when through trains ceased in 1916 and was finally closed in 1929, the platforms being too short for the new electric trains.

The remains of Ludgate Hill station are visible in the centre of this picture taken from the platform end at Holborn Viaduct. The tracks in the foreground are the very restricted station throat.

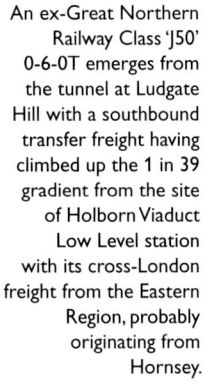

An ex-Great Northern Railway Class 'J50' 0-6-0T emerges from the tunnel at Ludgate Hill with a southbound transfer freight having climbed up the 1 in 39 gradient from the site of Holborn Viaduct Low Level station with its cross-London freight from the Eastern Region, probably originating from Hornsey.

Blackfriars

The original Blackfriars on the south bank of the river had been opened by the LC&DR as a temporary through station in 1864 but was closed in 1885 after the bridge over the Thames was completed. It was replaced by a new permanent station at Ludgate Hill, as part of the measures to reduce congestion at Ludgate Hill. The Thomas Cubitt-designed, 933 feet long, lattice girder bridge accommodated four tracks and it was supplemented in 1886 by a new bridge carrying seven tracks. At the northern end, it fanned out to carry the lines into a new terminus station which was known as St Pauls until February 1937 when it became Blackfriars. There were three terminal and two through platforms leading to Holborn Viaduct.

The station was completely rebuilt between 2009 and 2012 with the terminal platforms moved to the west side of the through platforms. All of them were extended onto the bridge to accommodate twelve car trains.

The original four-track lattice girder Blackfriars bridge in 1952, with the familiar dome of St Paul's Cathedral on the right. The bridge was dismantled in 1984-85 after it became corroded. *The Lens of Sutton Association*

This 1950s picture of the Blackfriars train shed shows the two through platforms viewed from the north of the station. All passenger trains to Holborn Viaduct called at Blackfriars but, by the 1960s, only a few peak-hour services used the terminal platforms. Empty stock for the evening peak-hour trains was berthed there during the day and worked via Metropolitan Junction to Cannon Street as required.

CHAPTER 1 - SOUTH EASTERN & CHATHAM RAILWAY STATIONS

'4-EPB' No. 5226 at Blackfriars in plain blue livery with full yellow ends, indicating a date in the late 1960s. These units were introduced in 1951, with a new type of self-lapping electro-pneumatic brake and new standard electrical equipment, hence the 'EPB' designation. The three terminal platforms at the station are all occupied, and visible on the left are the lattice girders of the original 1864 bridge.

Another '4-EPB', No. 5043 built in 1953, probably photographed on the same day as the picture above. The platforms were boarded to reduce their weight since they were built over the river. Blackfriars station was rebuilt in 1977 and became significantly busier when the Thameslink service started in the late 1980s.

Holborn Viaduct

Holborn Viaduct station was a quarter of a mile from the north bank of the Thames and was opened in 1874 by the LC&DR to relieve the pressure on Ludgate Hill. The latter could not be extended because of the high cost of land in the area and so a new terminus was built, abutting on to the newly constructed Holborn Viaduct, where the company already owned sufficient land and additional space was obtainable by building over the Metropolitan Extension line. The new station was at the end of a 264-yard spur from the Ludgate Hill-Farringdon line, with a frontage onto Holborn Viaduct. To the north was Smithfield Market, opened in 1868 and the largest wholesale meat market in Britain, and immediately to the east was the Old Bailey central criminal court.

The main station building was destroyed by bombing in the Second World War and the ruins remained for almost twenty years afterwards, as one of the many scars on the London landscape. It was finally rebuilt in 1963 and a new ten-storey office block was built above it. The station entrance and a new buffet were on the ground floor, although the barriers and platforms behind were left virtually unchanged.

In later years, Holborn Viaduct was only open during weekday rush-hours. It was closed completely in 1990 after the Thameslink cross city service through the re-opened tunnel to Farringdon began, and was replaced by a new through station, St Paul's Thameslink. The original Thameslink rail network was created by joining the electrified network south of the Thames with the then recently electrified line between Bedford and St Pancras to the north, via the Snow Hill tunnel. This allowed passengers to travel between stations to the north and south of London, including Bedford, Luton Airport, Gatwick Airport and Brighton, without changing trains or using the London Underground. Services began in 1988 and the route was fully inaugurated in May 1990.

This photograph, taken on 13th September 1956, shows the viaduct on to which the station abutted and its appalling condition in the post-war years. The van is delivering copies of *The Scotsman* newspaper. The pre-war 'Southern Electric' enamel signs on either side of the archway advertised, on the left, a 'Frequent service to Herne Hill, Peckham Rye, Crystal Palace, Catford, Wimbledon, South East and South West suburbs' and, on the right, 'Frequent trains to Herne Hill, Dulwich, Penge, Beckenham, Bromley, Bickley, Orpington'.

CHAPTER 1 - SOUTH EASTERN & CHATHAM RAILWAY STATIONS

A view showing the approach to Holborn Viaduct in the early 1950s, demonstrating the cramped nature of the site. The brick structure on the left is the long closed, single road engine shed, which was still there until at least 1985-86.

The lines dropping down the gradient on the left into a tunnel are to Snow Hill (renamed in 1912 as Holborn Viaduct Low Level) and Farringdon; those on the right are into the Holborn Viaduct terminus. The crossover was for the use of returning banking engines used to assist trains up the 1 in 39 gradient.

This is the old Holborn Viaduct signal box, which was situated above the lines down to West Street Junction, where the Smithfield Curve joined the line from Farringdon. It was fitted with a new electrical frame containing 86 levers for the introduction of colour light signalling as part of the 1926 electrification work. Together with a new box built at Blackfriars, these replaced seven manual boxes. Holborn Viaduct box was closed in March 1974, when it was replaced by a panel in Blackfriars signal box, facilitated by modern signalling equipment and the simplification of the track layout after the removal of Platforms 2 and 3 a year earlier.

The original platforms at Holborn Viaduct were short, the LC&DR designing them for half-length trains because it divided its Up services at Herne Hill into separate City and Victoria portions. The short Platforms 2, 3 and 6 were not electrified because, unlike Platforms 4 and 5, they could not be extended to take eight-car trains in 1925, when the station was being prepared for the introduction of electric services the following year. Platform 1 was not dealt with until 1939 when, at considerable expense, it was lengthened to accommodate an eight-car set. The three non-electrified platforms were used primarily for parcels traffic and were removed in 1973 and the track taken up. The overall roof of the station was dismantled in 1967.

A 1950s view of 1949-built '4-SUB' No. 4299 at Holborn Viaduct on a Sevenoaks service via the Catford Loop and Swanley. The building on the right, which adjoined the station, was occupied by Moores Modern Methods Ltd. Established in 1909, Moores supplied the British and many overseas governments, along with legal and accounting firms, with high grade leather filing/archiving binders, along with the forms that they held. Technological advancements saw the company diversify into the corporate gifts and promotional products industry, and it is still in business today, operating from Elstree in Hertfordshire.

The Lens of Sutton Association

On 19th November 1967, the Branch Line Society ran the 'East Kent Railtour', using a pair of BRC&W Type '3' diesels which 'topped and tailed' the train. No. D6595 was one of the narrow-bodied Hastings line locomotives, whilst No. D6585 was a standard version. No. D6595 brought the train from Victoria via Loughborough Junction and Blackfriars to Holborn Viaduct. The bomb-damaged station was finally rebuilt in 1963 with a ten-storey office block overhead, and this is visible above the train.

No. D6585 then headed the tour into Kent, travelling through London Bridge, Lewisham, Dartford, Gravesend, Rochester and Chatham to Sheerness. The trip continued around East Kent before returning to Victora via Folkestone, Ashford, Maidstone East, Swanley, Hither Green, Woolwich Arsenal, New Cross Gate, Sydenham, Crystal Palace, West Norwood, Streatham Hill and Balham. No. D6585 became No. 33065 under TOPS and carried the name *Sealion* between 1991 and 1996. It is now preserved at the Spa Valley Railway in Kent; No. D6595 was less fortunate and was cut up in 1990.

'4-EPB' No. 5236 at Holborn Viaduct in the early 1970s on a service to Orpington via Herne Hill. The cramped nature of the station is illustrated by the narrow platforms. Open only during weekday rush-hours in its later years, in 1989 the station was reduced to just Platforms 1 and 2, and closed completely in January 1990.

Holborn Viaduct Low Level

Until the end of the 20th Century, the former LC&DR link to the Metropolitan Railway at Farringdon Street was the only direct route across the centre of London. Its sharp curves and steep gradients meant that it was used only for freight traffic from 1916 onwards, until it was modernised and re-opened for passenger traffic in 1988, after the tunnel to Farringdon was re-opened as part of the Thameslink project.

A station was opened on the link line near Holborn Viaduct in 1874 to relieve the pressure on Ludgate Hill. It was originally called Snow Hill but this was changed to Holborn Viaduct Low Level in 1912. In May 1990, a new station, St Paul's Thameslink, was opened on the line, extending almost from Holborn Viaduct to Ludgate Hill and replacing the Holborn Viaduct terminus; it was renamed City Thameslink in 1991 to avoid confusion with the nearby St Paul's tube station.

On 13th September 1956, condenser fitted former Midland Railway Class '3F' 0-6-0T No. 47203 emerges into the daylight and passes the remains of Holborn Viaduct Low Level station, which had been closed since 1916. These engines were the precursors to the standard LM&SR 'Jinty' 0-6-0Ts. Built at Vulcan Foundry in December 1899, No. 47203 was allocated to Cricklewood from the late 1920s until April 1958, when it moved to Leicester Great Central. It would have been working a transfer freight from Brent sidings at Cricklewood to Bricklayers Arms. Note the ex-LC&DR lattice post signal to the left of the engine.

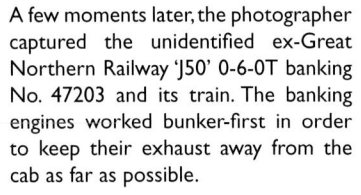

A few moments later, the photographer captured the unidentified ex-Great Northern Railway 'J50' 0-6-0T banking No. 47203 and its train. The banking engines worked bunker-first in order to keep their exhaust away from the cab as far as possible.

CHAPTER 1 - SOUTH EASTERN & CHATHAM RAILWAY STATIONS

Construction work in progress all around the remains of Holborn Viaduct Low Level station, as another condenser fitted Class '3F', No. 47248, is opened up to lift its train up the 1 in 39 incline towards Blackfriars. The 0-6-0T was built by Vulcan Foundry for the Midland Railway in June 1902 and was at Cricklewood from December 1946 until July 1962, when it moved north to Gorton for its final year in service. On the rear of the bunker, No. 47248 is displaying the inter-regional headlamp code for a train from the Midland lines to Herne Hill sidings.

Charing Cross

Charing Cross is the station closest to what most people consider the true centre of London. Its main entrance is on the Strand, a few yards away from Trafalgar Square and within a short distance of Whitehall. In 1859, the South Eastern Railway responded to the opening of Victoria station by the LB&SCR and the LC&DR, with a 1 mile 68 chain long line from the west end of London Bridge to Charing Cross via Waterloo, including a connection to the L&SWR at Waterloo. The cost was high, with the tracks carried on 190 brick arches, seventeen iron bridges and two iron viaducts. The River Thames was crossed on the lattice girder Hungerford Bridge, carrying four running lines and on the site of Isambard Kingdom Brunel's Charing Cross suspension bridge, the remains of which were sold and used for the Clifton suspension bridge in Bristol. The bridge had six 154 foot spans and three of 100 feet, and the company had to provide a footway alongside the tracks to replace the suspension bridge. The station, which opened in January 1864, had six platform faces and an arched roof similar to that built by the same designer at Cannon Street. It took over the main line services which had previously terminated at London Bridge, including the Continental boat trains.

In 1887, the bridge was widened to take three more tracks and after part of the roof collapsed in 1905, the station amenities were rebuilt and improved. The arched roof was replaced with a more modest affair using lattice girders supported on iron columns. There were various attempts in the first two decades of the 20th Century to strengthen the bridge and even to replace it with a road one, which would have resulted in the closure of the station. In 1936, the latter idea was finally dropped and the outbreak of the Second World War put paid to any further discussion on replacing the structure.

Electrification of the South Eastern suburban services in 1926 had relieved the loading pressure on it, by reducing the running lines over the oldest part of the bridge to two, with the other two becoming sidings. Minor improvements to the station's amenities were made over the following decades and extensive work was undertaken in 1954 to lengthen the platforms, so that they could all take ten-car trains. The Continental boat trains had ceased before the First World War and the station became primarily one for commuters, although main line services to Ramsgate, Folkestone and Dover via Tonbridge continue to run to this day.

A replica stone cross was commissioned for the station forecourt. The original Eleanor Cross, one of twelve erected at resting places for the body of Queen Eleanor as it was transported back from Lincolnshire to Westminster Abbey in 1290, had been destroyed in 1647.

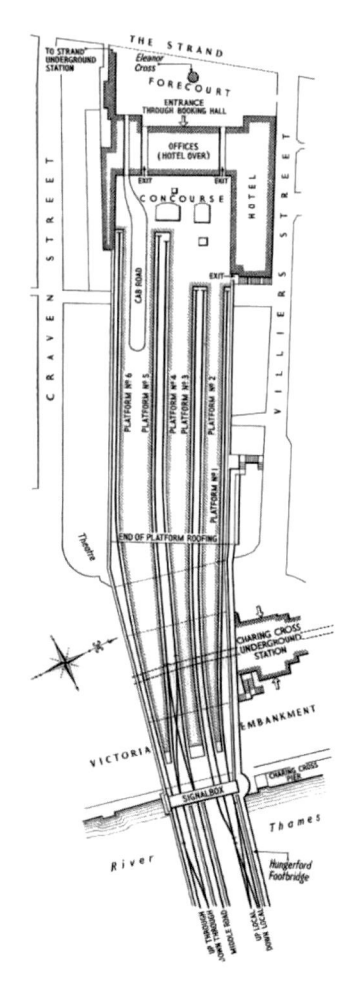

Above: Charing Cross, showing the forecourt as reduced by widening of The Strand in 1959.

Left: The original cast crest pictured here was replaced in 1985 by one made from polyester resin. When the station roof was rebuilt in 1906, it originally carried the letters SECR.

CHAPTER 1 - SOUTH EASTERN & CHATHAM RAILWAY STATIONS

Wainwright 'H' Class 0-4-4T No. 31162 on shunting and Empty Coaching Stock (ECS) duties at Charing Cross on 24th March 1951. It moved from Bricklayers Arms to Faversham by the end of June.

Two '4-SUB's at Charing Cross on 9th July 1952, with No. 4338 on the right, which was converted after the end of the war from a 1925 three-car '1496' Class with a new ten-compartment steel panelled trailer. The EMU in the centre carries the headcode 'O' for Orpington. Even before the platforms were extended for the ten-car trains in 1954, the narrowness at the end of Platforms 5 and 6 is noticeable. Platforms 5 and 6 were used for main line steam, and subsequently main line diesel and electric services. Both could handle twelve-car EMUs and Hastings DEMUs. Platform 6 could accommodate eleven-coach steam services with a main line engine at each end. The reason for the narrowness was the short siding to the left of platform 6, which was later abolished and the track slewed over, allowing the platform to be widened and slightly lengthened. The effect of this can be seen in the following pages.

'Battle of Britain' No. 34073 *249 Squadron* sets off from Charing Cross in the mid-1950s. It was built in May 1948 and repainted from its original Southern Railway malachite into British Railways green in December 1950. Its first allocation was Ramsgate, then Dover from January 1949 until May 1961.

Above left: The very narrow extended platform dating back to 1954 when Platforms 1 to 3 were lengthened to take ten-car trains. The track was laid on longitudinal timbers, as opposed to traditional transverse sleepers, due to the form of bridge construction and the need to spread axle loadings. This required constant monitoring and a high level of maintenance. The Royal Festival Hall dominates the skyline on the left. Charing Cross signal box, which spanned the approach tracks, had 107 levers in a power frame and was built in 1926 when four-aspect colour light signalling was installed. It closed in April 1976 when the London Bridge panel took over the area.

Above right: The entrance to the siding abolished to widen and lengthen Platforms 5/6 can be seen in the bottom right hand corner. Steam trains longer than ten coaches, where the engine would have fouled the crossover immediately at the exit from Platform 6, could depart via the scissors crossover halfway across the bridge instead, thus allowing them to occupy Platform 6 without fouling Platform 5 departures/arrivals. The scissors crossover in the foreground allowed up to eight-car EMUs to arrive/depart Platform 5 via the middle road, or similarly Platform 4 via the west side bridge, when operationally convenient or necessary.

Right: Ivatt LM&SR design Class '2' 2-6-2T No. 41299 on ECS duties at Charing Cross in the 1950s. The engine has backed onto an incoming train at Charing Cross and will take the stock out to Rotherhithe Road carriage sidings; note that the tail lamp had yet to be removed. No. 41299 entered service in November 1951, one of thirty of these engines built for the Southern Region. It went from new to Bricklayers Arms, and remained there until transferred to Exmouth Junction in February 1961.

CHAPTER 1 - SOUTH EASTERN & CHATHAM RAILWAY STATIONS

A Hastings line, narrow-bodied diesel-electric multiple unit waits in Platform 5 at Charing Cross. These units, the only main line DEMUs, were built in 1957 to work through the restricted tunnels between Tonbridge and Hastings. The six-car sets were powered by a 500hp English Electric diesel in each power car driving standard electric traction motors. The first seven sets were built on short 56ft 11in underframes, the traditional length of Hastings line coaching stock, and had 8ft wide bodies. Once their initial noise and vibration problems were overcome, they settled down to a give a very acceptable level of service for many years.

Twenty of the 'Schools' Class 4-4-0s were fitted with the Lemaître multiple jet exhaust enclosed in a large diameter chimney, including No. 30934 *St.Lawrence* in 1940, pictured backing out of Platform 6 in April 1957. It was allocated to Bricklayers Arms from new in March 1935, remaining there until June 1959 when it was transferred to Ashford. The platforms at Charing Cross extended out onto Hungerford Bridge.

No. 30913 *Christ's Hospital* waits to depart with the 8.20pm to Hastings on 12th April 1958. The 'Schools' was in lined black from January 1952 until June 1959 and it was allocated to Ramsgate from April 1945 until June 1959, when it moved to the Western section at Nine Elms following the inauguration of the first part of the Kent Coast electrification scheme. This was an example of a Ramsgate 'Schools' on a Hastings diagram, working one of the South Eastern section's sometimes complex circular runs, the locomotive eventually returning home from Hastings via Ashford, where it would turn, and then on via Dover or Canterbury West.

The Hastings trains were all converted to DEMU operation by June 1958 and No. 30910 *Merchant Taylors* hauled the last 8.20pm Charing Cross to Hastings on 7th June. It had been repainted from lined black to green in August 1956 and was allocated to Ramsgate from June 1957 until June 1959, moving to Nine Elms with most of the other steam locomotives displaced by the Kent Coast electrification. In the right foreground, the outline of the earlier narrow platform, prior to the siding being abolished and the platform widened, shows up clearly.

The second '4-EPB' set, No. 5002 built in 1951, is seen here in all-blue livery in the 1970s at Charing Cross. Note that the cast crest, which was positioned between the 'S' and 'R', has disappeared; it was not replaced until 1985.

The rear of '2-HAP' No. 6105, with a red tail light in the headcode box, heading out across Hungerford Bridge towards Waterloo Eastern in the 1970s. The BR-design '2-HAP' units were introduced in 1957-58 to replace Southern Railway 'HAL' stock, and for use on the Thanet lines in Kent after electrification. They comprised an 'EPB' type motor coach coupled to a driving trailer composite. The 107-lever Charing Cross signal box dated from June 1926, when its power frame replaced a mechanical lever signal box. The box was closed in April 1976 when the London Bridge panel took over. Note that the scissors crossover between Platforms 4 and 5 shown in the earlier photographs had been removed, because it was not extensively used and was limited to a maximum of eight-car units. The first coach of the twelve car 'CEP/BEP' EMU for Ramsgate on the right is protruding beyond the ramp of Platform 6.

'Battle of Britain' No. 34078 222 *Squadron* approaching Waterloo Eastern station on 26th March 1959, with Hungerford Bridge and Charing Cross in the distance. It is heading 'The Man of Kent', the 1.10 pm from Charing Cross to Folkestone, Dover, Deal, Ramsgate and Margate, running with carriage nameboards but no headboard. No. 34078 was built in July 1948 and never rebuilt; it retained the tender 'raves' until withdrawn in September 1964. In the centre background, the Royal Festival Hall is partly obscured by construction work in front. The Shot Tower, used for many years in the production of gunshot – allowing drops of molten lead to solidify as they were dropped into a water tank at the base of the tower – is just visible above the column of smoke from the engine.

CHAPTER 1 - SOUTH EASTERN & CHATHAM RAILWAY STATIONS

Waterloo Eastern

The approaches to Waterloo Eastern, looking from the platforms at the east end of the station, with the bridge carrying the line into Blackfriars in the background. It was opened by the South Eastern Railway in 1869 as Waterloo Junction, renamed Waterloo Eastern in July 1935 and Waterloo East in May 1977. Originally, there was a connecting line from the SER into the L&SWR Waterloo terminus but this was taken out of use in 1911.

'4-SUB' No. 4136 at Waterloo Eastern on 1st August 1951, in early British Railways livery with large unit number prefixed with a small 'S'. This was one of the augmented '4-SUB' units dating from the mid-1940s, produced from a '3-SUB' with the addition of a similar pattern trailer car. Code 'V' was for London and Dartford via Greenwich (in the Down direction this would apply from either Charing Cross or Cannon Street but in the Up direction a Charing Cross service would also display a bar over the 'V').

Lens of Sutton Association

'4-EPB' No. 5106 arriving at Waterloo Eastern with a Charing Cross to Hayes via Lewisham service on 17th March 1964. The enamel warning sign, based closely on a Southern Railway sign, is headed 'The Railway Executive', which came into being upon Nationalisation but was abolished with effect from 1st October 1953.

One of the six-car, narrow-bodied, diesel-electric multiple units built in 1957 for the Charing Cross/Cannon Street-Hastings service, No. 1002 at Waterloo Eastern in the 1970s. This was one of the first seven units built on short 56ft 11in underframes; the sixteen subsequent units had 63ft 6in underframes. Its '22' headcode for a Charing Cross to Hastings via Orpington and Battle train had not been set correctly and is displaying only the top of the left hand '2'. Note also that the canopy over Platform D at Waterloo Eastern was being shortened at this time; it remains much shorter to this day.

Borough Market and Metropolitan Junctions
This triangular junction was carried on a series of bridges and viaducts, with Borough Market directly below it, whilst just to the north of the lines is Southwark Cathedral. To the east, the end of the platforms at London Bridge were less than 300 yards away, Cannon Street to the north was immediately across the river and to the west was the route to Charing Cross via Metropolitan Junction and Waterloo (Eastern). Signal boxes at Cannon Street, Metropolitan Junction and Borough Market Junction controlled the movements through the junction with four-aspect colour lights. Around 1,000 trains per day passed over the junction – less than the 2,400 at Clapham Junction but there they were not over conflicting paths like those at Borough Market. In May 1932, the junction had been re-laid with expensive but more durable manganese steel rail, in place of the usual carbon steel, such was the intensity of the traffic passing over it. Even so, the point switches had to be renewed at less than two yearly intervals.

An innovative solution was introduced in 1922 to the operational constraint imposed by the junction, in the form of 'parallel' running between London Bridge and Cannon Street, with two trains running out from the terminus at the same time as two ran in, and vice versa. It used two basic principles: at junction points, Up and Down trains on the same routes passed at the same times, thereby avoiding conflicting movements; where multiple tracks were available, pairs of both Up and Down trains were scheduled to run parallel in non-conflicting paths. Thus two Up trains departing simultaneously from Platforms 7 and 4 or 6 at London Bridge for Cannon Street could both be given clear parallel paths through Borough Market Junction. In the other direction, two Down services were scheduled to pass the junction at the same time as the two Up trains. The trains were routed to or from platforms at Cannon Street so that all four had clear paths between the two stations. In the middle of these two pairs of two trains, two Charing Cross services were also dealt with. An Up train from London Bridge could diverge at Borough Market Junction, and at the same time a Down train from Charing Cross pass, this avoiding any conflict with any of the four Cannon Street services.

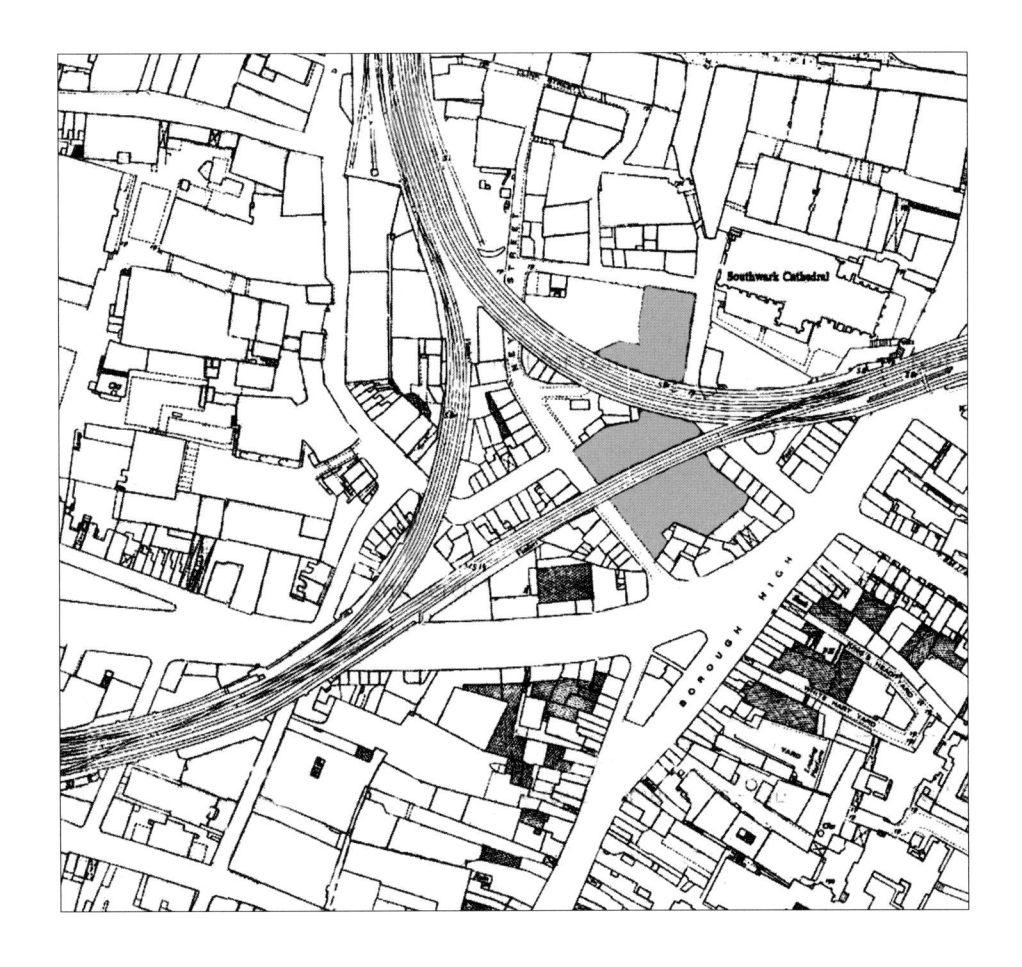

Left: '2-EPB' No. 5721 on a Charing Cross to Sevenoaks service illustrates the parallel working through the junction. During the existence of Borough Market Junction signal box, the arrangement was, from left to right, Up-Up-Down-Down. Two Up and two Down trains could run to/from Cannon Street simultaneously or, as here, one Up and one Down Charing Cross plus a Down Cannon Street. Anything else conflicted.

Below: All of the tracks around the junction were built on bridges, viaducts and arches. Looking from a busy Borough High Street in the early 1970s, part of Southwark Cathedral is just visible on the right before the bridge and Borough Market Junction signal box can be seen on the viaduct.

This picture, taken on 13th March 1957, shows how the line to Cannon Street squeezed through the crowded Borough Market area. There was a permanent 20mph speed restriction around the check-railed, seven-chain radius curve. On the left is Southwark Cathedral, only twenty yards from the railway viaduct built in 1862 and the oldest cathedral church building in London, with parts dating back to at least the 13th century. Until 1905, it was the parish church of St. Saviour, becoming Southwark Cathedral when the Church of England Diocese of Southwark was created. The area of Borough can be traced back to around 1000 AD and it developed for centuries around the only crossing point over the river, London Bridge. The site occupied by the original local market was purchased by the parishioners of St. Saviour's in 1754. During the 19th Century it developed as a wholesale market but, after peaking in the 1930s, began a decline which increased as supermarkets developed after the Second World War and the importance of the wholesaler reduced. This was completed by the opening of New Covent Garden wholesale market at Vauxhall in 1974 and its building lay empty for many years. However, in the late 1990s Borough Market's fortunes were revived as artisan foods became fashionable, and it is now open six days a week and attracts thousands of visitors each year. The roofs of some of the market buildings are visible between the Cathedral and the parapet of the viaduct, and Borough Market Junction signal box is in the centre background.

RC Riley/The Transport Treasury

Looking towards London Bridge as a 'Schools' 4-4-0 approaches with ECS for Charing Cross, also on 13th March 1957. The reason for using a tender-first main line locomotive like this was that once it had been released from the stop blocks, it could then take out a subsequent main line service having reached the station without occupying a scarce path, particularly important during the rush hour. Borough Market Junction signal box, on the left, was in continuous use for forty-eight years until the start of the London Bridge Signalling scheme in April 1976. It had a miniature lever frame containing thirty-five levers and was double-manned for most of the day. It handled forty-one Up and forty-eight Down trains daily between 5pm and 6pm in the late 1940s. Since its decommissioning in 1976, the wooden upper part of the box has been on display at the National Railway Museum in York. Note the window cleaning balcony.
RC Riley/The Transport Treasury

This aerial view of Borough Market and the triangular junction in the 1970s shows how the tracks were threaded through the surrounding area. Southwark Cathedral is on the right and Borough Market itself underneath the railway. The tracks to the left go to Waterloo Eastern and Charing Cross, on the right to Cannon Street across the Thames, and those at the bottom of the picture to London Bridge. There are three EMUs, two making their way around the junction and the third parked in the siding at the end of Cannon Street Bridge.

Colin Marsden

Cannon Street

A shuttle service ran to Charing Cross, and the Greenwich line trains were extended from London Bridge. Initially, Cannon Street was served by almost all trains to and from Charing Cross but these ceased in 1916. Increased traffic resulted in a widening of the approach viaduct to accommodate ten tracks, and an additional platform was added.

When the Southern Railway electrified the former South Eastern Railway suburban lines in the mid-1920s, the opportunity was taken to re-arrange the track layout at Cannon Street to eliminate conflicting movements as far as possible, and to allow parallel operation of trains to and from London Bridge. Four-aspect colour light signalling was installed, the engine shed and turntable were taken out, and the number of turnouts was reduced by twenty-four, from 101 to seventy-seven.

In 1939, 16,500 passengers departed from the station in the peak rush hour. By 1959, this had increased to 23,500 following lengthening of the platforms in 1955 to take longer trains when the Southern Region undertook a major investment programme to allow a twenty-five per cent increase in train capacity, by allowing the use of ten cars instead of eight. The cost of the work at Cannon Street alone was £1.25 million. In 1967, 40,800 passengers arrived each day, 38,300 of them between 7am and 10am, and 38,100 departed between 4pm and 8pm out of a total of 39,200.

Suburban trains ran to Charing Cross throughout the day but there was only a limited suburban service to Cannon Street off-peak. Main line trains used Charing Cross off-peak but, apart from a handful of Hastings services, all other peak-hour main line trains used Cannon Street.

The distinctive iron roof was demolished between April 1958 and January 1959, the two acres of glass having been taken out during the war following bomb damage. The platforms were extended to take twelve coach trains by extending Platforms 5 to 8 out onto the bridge. Despite plans to rebuild the station, the redevelopment was only partly completed by the mid-1960s, with a fifteen-storey office block replacing Southern House, the former Cannon Street Hotel converted into offices in 1931, which had been found to be structurally unsound; a concrete apron covered the inner ends of the platforms. The City Corporation remodelled the roads around the station and this required replacement of the approach bridge, which was followed by the provision of umbrella type canopies over the exposed platform ends.

Eventually, the station was completely rebuilt, firstly with two six-storey office blocks built over the platforms in the late 1980s, and then in 2011 the concourse and old office block were replaced with Cannon Place, a mixed-use office/retail development incorporating the entrance to the station. All that remains of the original building are the two Grade II listed towers which were restored by the Railway Heritage Trust in 1986.

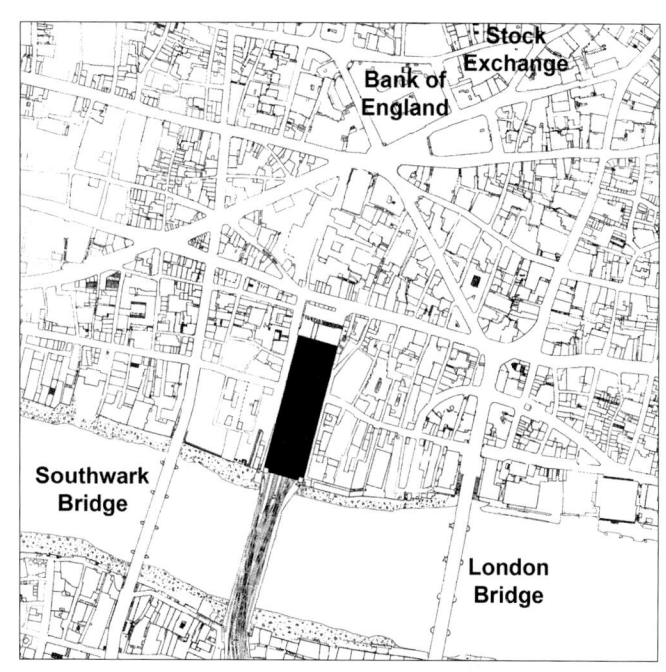

Above: Cannon Street was opened on the north bank of the Thames in 1866 as the City station of the South Eastern Railway, in response to the authorisation of the extension of the rival LC&DR to Ludgate Hill. It was reached by a 60-chain branch from the Charing Cross line to the west of London Bridge via a triangular junction at Borough Market. The line crossed the river on five approach tracks using a new bridge before branching into nine platform roads. Space constraints forced the station building to abut right up to the bridge. The train shed was covered by a massive almost semi-circular 190ft span roof, 680ft in length, and at the river end there were two arcaded towers.

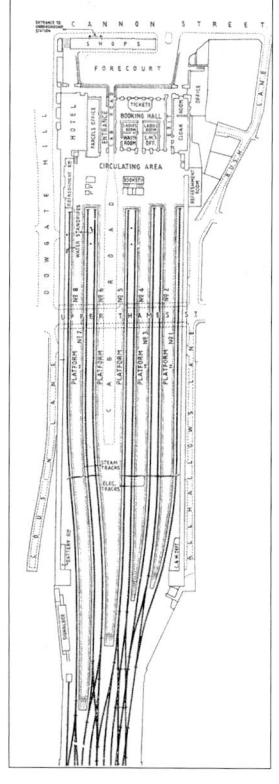

Right: The station layout from 1926 until the late 1960s. In 1955, Platforms 1 to 5 had been extended into the concourse for the ten-car suburban scheme, whilst in around 1957-58 Platforms 5 to 8 were extended out onto the bridge to take twelve-car EMUs for the forthcoming Ramsgate/Dover via Chatham electrification and Hastings DEMUs.

Right: A view showing both the great height of the roof compared with the size of the EMU below and the intricate detail of the arcaded towers topped by weather vanes and the ironwork supporting the overall roof. The two acres of glass in the massive roof were taken out during the war following bomb damage and never replaced.

The approach to Cannon Street over the river bridge, showing the track layout as remodelled in 1926 when the Southern Railway electrified the former South Eastern Railway suburban lines. The opportunity was taken to re-arrange the layout to eliminate conflicting movements as far as possible, and to allow parallel operation of trains to and from London Bridge. Four-aspect colour light signalling was installed and the number of turnouts was reduced by a quarter to seventy-seven. In the distance, an EMU departs from the station. The middle engine siding shown here was abolished when Platforms 5 to 8 were extended over the bridge to take twelve-car trains in 1957-58.

Unusually, four steam locomotives outnumber the EMUs by two to one in this early 1950s picture of Cannon Street, taken before the demolition of the bomb-damaged roof.

CHAPTER 1 - SOUTH EASTERN & CHATHAM RAILWAY STATIONS

No. 34078 *222 Squadron* arriving at Cannon Street with the 7.19am from Ramsgate on 9th July 1958. Built in July 1948 and never rebuilt, No. 34078 retained the tender side 'raves' until withdrawn in September 1964, the only one of the class to retain a 5,500 gallon tender in this form until the end. It has the wider cab, introduced from No. 34071 onwards. No. 34078 was also the only original Bulleid Pacific ever allocated to Bricklayers Arms, the other fifteen on its books being rebuilds. The archway and steps on Bankside, leading up to the south end of Southwark Bridge, can be seen on the right of the picture.

Two '4-EPB's at a quiet Cannon Street during the middle of the day. Although suburban trains ran to Charing Cross throughout the day, there was only a limited suburban service to Cannon Street in the off-peak hours. Main line trains used Charing Cross off-peak but, except for a handful of Hastings line services, all other peak-hour main line trains used Cannon Street. The unit on the right is displaying Code '9' for a Cannon Street to Bromley North via Parks Bridge service.

No. 30772 Sir Percivale, nicknamed 'Percy' by the regular commuters, at Cannon Street with the 5.40pm to Dover on 12th July 1956. Hither Green shed always turned out an immaculate 'King Arthur' for this train, Duty '182' which was its only passenger duty, although its balancing working was the less glamorous 12.50am goods. This was the last of the steam-hauled business trains from Cannon Street to be restored after the war. Hither Green only had one 'King Arthur', especially for this train; a Bricklayers Arms or Ashford 'King Arthur' was not used. The 'King Arthur' came off at Ashford before returning to Hither Green with the 9.55pm freight, arriving at 1.23am the next day. This gave the shed cleaners the whole morning and the early afternoon to groom it before it turned and went off shed to Cannon Street at 3.30pm to work the empty seven coach train from Grove Park into Charing Cross. Just before 5pm, a 'Schools' from Ramsgate shed would couple onto the train and work it tender-first, with the 'King Arthur' still attached, round to Cannon Street. Sir Percivale was one of the 'Scotch Arthurs', built by the North British Locomotive Company in June 1925 and was at Hither Green from August 1954 until June 1957, when it was transferred to Bournemouth. The signal box on the left was severely damaged in 1957 when a fire broke out in the relay room. It had been built in 1926 as part of the introduction of colour light signalling, replacing Cannon Street No. 1 box which had been the largest manual box in the country with 243 levers. It was 45 feet long and contained a 143-lever frame.

CHAPTER 1 - SOUTH EASTERN & CHATHAM RAILWAY STATIONS

'Schools' 4-4-0s based at Bricklayers Arms shed were staple motive power on the Hastings trains from Cannon Street, until the advent of the diesel-electric multiple units in 1957-58. No. 30935 *Sevenoaks* was allocated there from new in 1935 and apart from nine months at St. Leonards in 1949-50, it remained there until June 1959. It received BR lined green livery at the end of 1956.

'King Arthur' No. 30796 *Sir Dodinas le Savage* on Hither Green Duty '182', the 5.47pm to Dover (previously the 5.40pm that had been retimed from June 1957). The 5.47pm had been worked by a Class 'N' 2-6-0 for a time but for the final few weeks No. 30796 was used and it took a packed ten-coach train from Cannon Street on the last steam-hauled train on Friday 6th June 1958. No. 30796 was built at Eastleigh in April 1926 and was allocated to Hither Green between June 1957 and June 1959.

Two views of No. 34004 *Yeovil* ready for departure from Cannon Street with the 12.45pm SO to Ramsgate on 30th May 1959. The headcode indicates it is routed over the Dartford Loop line (via Sidcup) to Dartford, then via Gravesend, Strood and Chatham due to re-signalling in the Chislehurst area, in connection with the North Kent 1959 main line electrification scheme. The rebuilt 'Pacific' is framed by the two towers which were Grade II listed in 1972; the one on the right housed a water tank that provided hydraulic power and water for locomotives. The overall iron roof had been removed at the start of the year, leaving the two towers in splendid isolation.

Yeovil was well-known for its exploits on the Highland Line in Scotland during the 1948 Locomotive Interchange Trials, where it put up some tremendous work, albeit at the expense of heavy fuel consumption. It had been rebuilt, completed in January 1958, and worked until the bitter end of SR steam in July 1967. No. 34004 was allocated to Bricklayers Arms after rebuilding, having been at Exmouth Junction from new in 1945, and was transferred to Stewarts Lane in February 1961, before moving to the Western section three months later. The short replacement canopies added when the overall roof was taken down are just visible on the extreme right.

'West Country' No. 34012 *Launceston* departing from Cannon Street on Friday 12th June 1959, the last weekday of steam operation to Ramsgate. The following Monday the trains would be worked by new '4-CEP' EMU stock. The engine was one of seven light 'Pacifics' which went to Bricklayers Arms after rebuilding, in this case in February 1958, and eight more followed on closure of Ramsgate shed in June 1959, together with unrebuilt No. 34078. *Launceston* stayed at Bricklayers Arms for over four years, leaving for Brighton in July 1962. It was transferred to Salisbury in September 1963 and finally to Bournemouth in October 1965, being withdrawn in December 1966 and cut up at Cashmore's scrapyard in Newport. In the background is Tower Bridge and the rows of cranes on either side of the river which were famously lowered in sequence as a tribute to Sir Winston Churchill, as his coffin was taken up the Thames from St. Paul's to Waterloo station in January 1965.

Blue-liveried '2-EPB' No. 5774 at the head of a Cannon Street to Orpington train on 12th July 1972. Over ten years had passed since the roof had been demolished in 1959 but little had changed in the intervening time, with the old station walls and the tower untouched. Eventually, in the late 1980s, the station was completely rebuilt leaving the now Grade II listed towers as the only link with the past.

Park Street

'West Country' No. 34017 *Ilfracombe* waits in Park Street siding on the south of the river in around 1959. There was no space either here or at Cannon Street for any servicing facilities, so engines went to be turned, coaled and watered at Ewer Street, an outpost of Bricklayers Arms shed situated between Borough Market Junction and the 'Grande Vitesse' or continental freight depot on the line towards Waterloo; it remained in use until around 1961. Ewer Street turntable could not accommodate anything larger than a 'Schools', so larger engines had to be turned on the Borough Market Junction-Cannon Street-Metropolitan Junction triangle, then serviced at Ewer Street. The Barclay Perkins & Co. Anchor brewery can be seen in the background behind No. 34017. The brewery was established in 1616 and by 1809 it had an annual output of 260,000 barrels, making it the largest in the world. Barclay Perkins was an early adopter of lager production in the UK with the Anchor brewing lager from 1922. In 1955, Barclay Perkins merged with rival London brewer Courage. Brewing continued at the Anchor site until the early 1970s but in 1981 the brewery buildings were demolished. *Ilfracombe* was rebuilt in late 1957 and was allocated to Bricklayers Arms from June 1959 until January 1961 when it was transferred to Nine Elms, from where it was withdrawn in October 1966.

London Bridge
London Bridge is the oldest of the permanent termini, dating back to the opening of London's first passenger railway in 1836, the London & Greenwich Railway. The L&GR was far-sighted because it built the viaduct over which the station was approached with space for eight tracks and, within six years, the London & Croydon Railway, the South Eastern Railway and the London & Brighton Railway were all using the station.

A new enlarged joint station was opened in February 1844 but, when the L&GR attempted to increase the running charges it levied on the other companies, the South Eastern Railway decided to build its own terminus at Bricklayers Arms. However, this was poorly situated and by 1852 had become a goods depot. In 1845, the SER took over the L&GR on lease, the latter remaining a separate undertaking until 1923. The new joint station was already proving to be too small and was demolished in 1849. The SER erected a boundary wall down the centre of the terminal site and built its own terminus on the north side. Over the next few years there were further piecemeal developments by each of the users but the most important development was the Charing Cross extension of the SER, which had to turn sharply to the south-west as soon as it left the SER part of the station. Extensive alterations were required to convert the terminal to a through station, the work being completed in January 1864. The southern part of the SER station was converted into an eight road Continental goods depot. This meant that there were now effectively three stations at London Bridge – the through station used by the Eastern Section, the terminus station of the Central Section and the small, so-called 'Low Level' station between them.

The LB&SCR side of the station was the next to be redeveloped, in response to increasing traffic requirements, eventually being completely rebuilt in 1893-94; it had eleven platform lines. The Continental goods depot was moved to Southwark in 1899 and was replaced by four Low Level terminal platforms.

In 1901, two additional tracks were added to the approach viaduct by the newly constituted South Eastern & Chatham Railway, making a total of eleven parallel tracks, eight serving the SE&CR and three for the LB&SCR. In 1909, the first electric service began, over the South London line to Victoria via Denmark Hill. After the 1923 Grouping, the Southern Railway electrified all of the former South Eastern Railway suburban lines by 1926, in addition to converting the 6,600 volt single-phase ac overhead lines to 600 volt dc third rail in 1929.

In 1928, there was a rather symbolic change when an opening was made in the wall between the two sides of the station, by now referred to as 'Eastern' and 'Central', together with a new footbridge to help passenger interchange across the station. Operational arrangements were also reorganised to reduce crossing movements and the approach tracks were rearranged. A final change was the renumbering of the twenty-one platforms, although Platform 5 never existed and was a light engine road between Platforms 4 and 6.

There was little change after 1928, except for the removal in 1936 of the turntable opposite the ends of Platforms 15 and 16, the steam engines being sent to New Cross Gate for turning, and the extension of most of the platforms to accommodate longer trains. By that date the station was handling around 250,000 passengers each day, of which around 170,000 went through the barriers, and there were over 2,400 train movements in each twenty-four hours; in the morning peak ninety-four trains arrived, of which nineteen continued to Charing Cross and to Cannon Street.

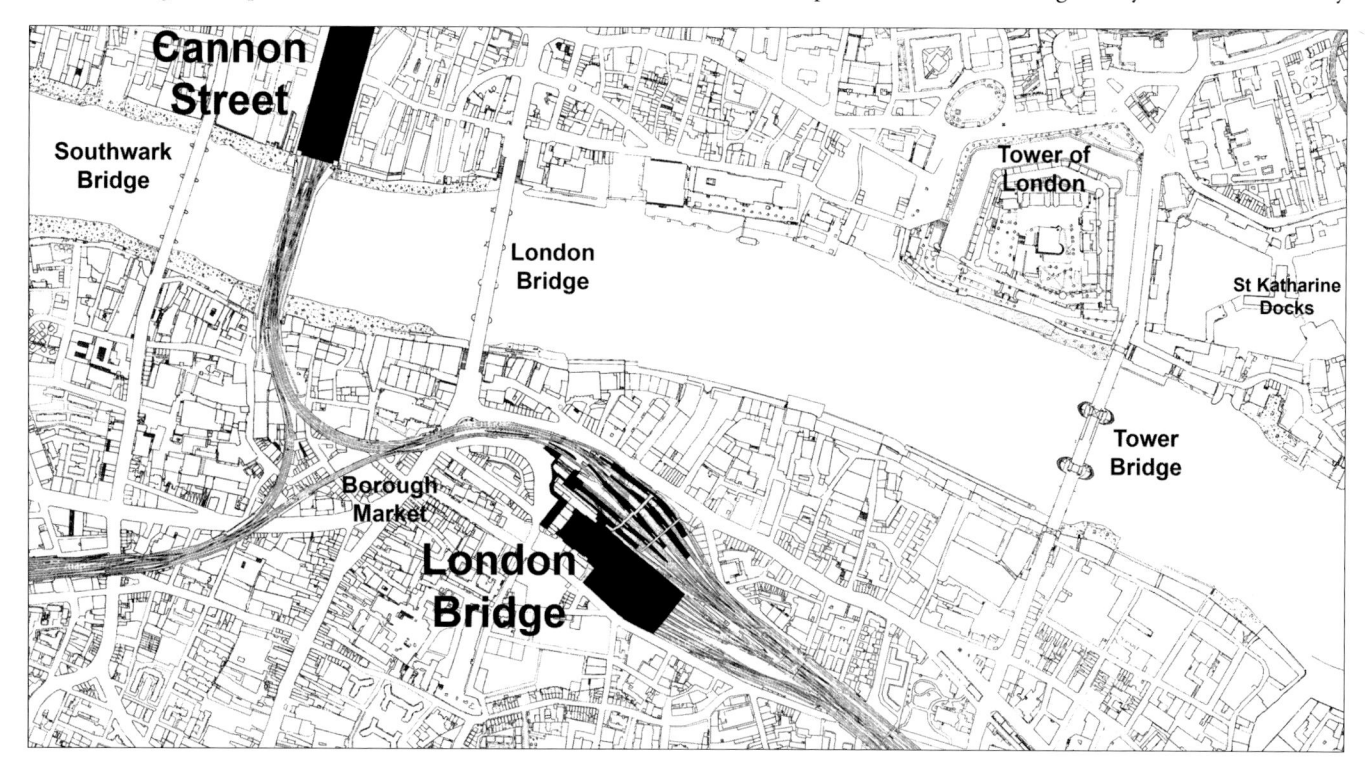

In British Railways days, the traffic at the station remained concentrated in the rush hour, with 61,400 passenger arrivals between 7am and 10am, out of a daily total of 86,300 in 1967. The Low Level platforms were therefore generally closed each weekday between 10am and 3pm, and at weekends. The Central Section station was used by suburban services throughout the day but the only off-peak main line services were hourly Brighton stopping trains (all stations south of Purley via Redhill), usually operated by '4-LAV' units.

In 1972, under the working title 'Operation London Bridge', the Southern Region began a major reconstruction of the station and surrounding lines. It included new signalling covering the routes from Charing Cross and Cannon Street out to Eltham and Bromley, and from London Bridge to Clapham, controlled from a panel box brought into use in mid-1975. There was a new concourse, footbridge and subway, platforms 20 to 22 were closed and a fifteen-storey office block built by a private developer was opened; the work was completed in April 1976. Almost forty years later, in 2012, work started on a fundamental rebuilding of London Bridge and its approaches. When completed in 2018, the station will have nine through platforms and six terminating platforms, and a massive concourse from which all platforms can be accessed.

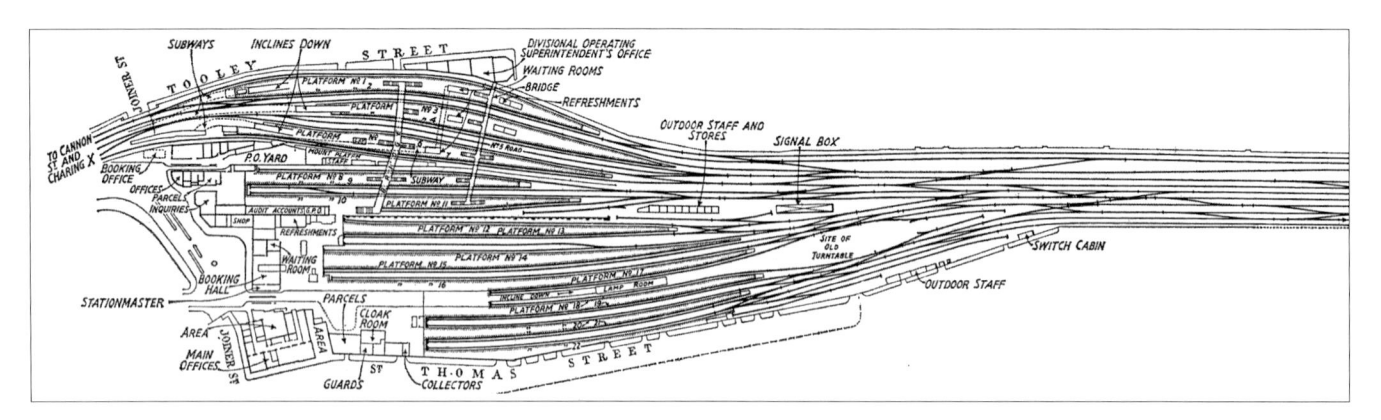

Above: On the right, eleven tracks entered the station from the south, and on the left, four from Cannon Street and Charing Cross through Borough Market Junction. The curved island Platforms 1 and 2, 3 and 4, 6 and 7 were the 'Through' or 'High Level' SE&CR station. Platform 5 never existed and was a light engine road between Platforms 4 and 6. Platforms 1, 2 and 3 were for Down trains and Platform 4 could be used for Down worrking in adverse weather conditions by trains terminating in it. Main line trains to the Kent coast used Platform 3 in the Down direction, and Platforms 6 and 7 in the Up. Opposite Platform 7 and sharing the same road was the 'Mount', a short low platform used for parcels traffic. Platforms 8 to 11 were the SE&CR 'Low Level' terminus, used for parcels traffic and rush-hour trains. The short 393ft long Platform 11 was not electrified and was normally used for stabling vans and locomotives. The LB&SCR terminus station platforms were numbered 12 to 22. Platforms 12 and 13 were used for suburban services, the long Platforms 14 to 16 for South Coast main-line trains of up to twelve-cars, and Platforms 17 to 22 for suburban trains, with 19 to 22 referred to as the South London Line platforms.

Left: London Bridge looking from Borough Market in the late 1940s, showing how sharply the Charing Cross extension of the South Eastern Railway had to turn to the south west as soon as it left the station.

London Bridge was approached from the south by eleven parallel tracks built on viaducts. The tracks on the left of the signal box led to the former LB&SCR terminus station. Immediately to the right of the box were the lines into the 'Low Level' SE&CR platforms, and out of picture on the right were the SE&CR through platforms. London Bridge signal box dated back to 1928 and was a non-standard, three-storey, all-brick structure, although built to a similar outline as the Southern Railway Type '11' and '12' designs. It was fitted with a 311-lever Westinghouse Brake & Saxby Signal Co. Ltd frame, which controlled 216 signals and seventy-nine sets of points. The box was closed in April 1976 when signalling of the area was taken over by London Bridge Area Signal Centre. The spire on the left of the picture is on the top of the medical block of Guy's Hospital, and the modern building in front is New Guy's House, the surgical centre built in the 1950s.

An ex-LB&SCR Marsh 'Atlantic', probably No. 32422 *North Foreland*, at Platform 17, one of the 'Brighton' terminal roads, at London Bridge in 1952. in the left background, an EMU picks its way over the approach trackwork from the south.

Moving in closer to look at the ex-LB&SCR terminal platforms which had been completely rebuilt in 1893-94 and was much more spacious than the SE&CR side of the station. An EMU on an afternoon London Bridge to Tattenham Corner Central section service waits at Platform 14.

Ex-SE&CR Wainwright 'C' Class 0-6-0 No. 31090 still has 'SOUTHERN' on the tender as it enters Platform 7 with an Up Continental van train on 17th April 1952. Built in 1903 at Ashford and allocated to Bricklayers Arms when photographed, it was withdrawn from there in August 1953. On the left, the 'ghost' Platform No. 5 road is still in place. The coaches to the right are a 60ft SE&CR 'Birdcage' set with a Brake Lavatory Third (formerly Second/Third Composite Brake) furthest from the camera. Note the roof detail; roofs were constructed by placing longitudinal planks over ribs (roof hoops), and what seems to have happened here is that the white lead painted over the canvas covering has worn to the point where water has got into and expanded the stopping between the planks, resulting in the prominent ridges shown in the photograph.

L&NER-built 'J50' 0-6-0T No. 68930 from Hornsey shed with a northbound inter-regional freight from Hither Green to the Eastern Region via Farringdon on 27th June 1956. Note the headcode on the rear of the bunker displaying three lamps; this was one of the special codes used to denote an inter-regional working across London. No. 68930 is climbing the 1 in 103 gradient into Platform 7, one of the through lines to Borough Market Junction. On the left is the space where the No. 5 light engine road had been until late 1952. The approach lines to the four low-level ex-SE&CR terminal platforms are on the right, whilst the former LB&SCR lines are off picture to the right of the signal box and water tower.

Outside the rush-hour peak, the Low Level platforms at London Bridge were used for parcels and mail traffic, as illustrated by 'E1' No. 31165 as it leaves with the 'Midday Vans' in May 1953. It was built in 1907 at Ashford as an SE&CR 'E' Class 4-4-0 and was one of ten engines rebuilt to an 'E1' by Beyer, Peacock in 1920, following the successful modification of one of the class in 1919. The appearance of the engine was significantly changed, as is evident if compared with No. 31166 in original condition on the following page. The footplate over the driving wheels was raised and the Wainwright cab was replaced with a standard Maunsell type. A new larger firebox was fitted and the slide valves were replaced with long-travel piston valves. No. 31165 had recently been transferred from Stewarts Lane to Bricklayers Arms and was withdrawn from there in 1959. The second vehicle of the parcels train is of North Eastern Railway design, although probably built in early L&NER days.

A month after the picture on the previous page of No. 31165, 'E' Class 4-4-0 No. 31166 was on the same duty. It has no smokebox numberplate and the number 31166 has been painted on the buffer beam in Southern Railway style. Allocated to Faversham at this date, No. 31166 spent much of the year in store before it was transferred to Tonbridge in October 1953; it was withdrawn from there in May 1955.

Tender-first 'Schools' No. 30911 *Dover* in the 1950s at London Bridge Platform 4, which was signalled for reversible running. It was allocated to Ramsgate from June 1952 until June 1959, moving to Nine Elms as part of the mass clear-out of steam after the Kent Coast electrification was switched on. There are two options for what is shown here. No. 30911 may have been on its way from Rotherhithe Road carriage sidings to Charing Cross or Cannon Street, in which case the main line train engine would have dragged both the stock and No. 30911 (which would have run light engine from Bricklayers Arms and been attached at Rotherhithe Road) and then reversed once on the main line in the North Kent Junction area. The 'Schools' would then have dragged the train and its main line engine to the terminus. The other option was that this could be stock being taken from Stewarts Lane to Cannon Street via Brixton Junction/Nunhead to Blackheath by the main train engine and reversing there, with No. 30911 attached to drag the whole lot back into Cannon Street. All this was done to avoid light engine's using paths in the rush hour.

'Schools' 4-4-0 No. 30904 *Lancing* at London Bridge Platform 1 with a Hastings service on 4th February 1954. It is in BR lined black livery, which it carried from September 1949 until July 1958 when it was repainted in lined green. *Lancing* was allocated to St Leonards shed from 1933 until June 1957.

Built as a 'C2' in 1902 and rebuilt in 1912 as a 'C2X', No. 32546 with a permanent way train in Platform 13 at London Bridge in the 1950s. The 'C2' was R.J. Billinton's first main line 0-6-0 goods locomotive for the LB&SCR. In 1908, Billinton's successor, D.E. Marsh, rebuilt three of the class with improved boilers and they were reclassified as 'C2X'. Another 'C2' was rebuilt in 1909 and a further twenty-seven up to 1922, including No. 32546 in 1912, with a final ten by the SR in 1924-25. No. 32546 was allocated to Norwood Junction from 1949 until withdrawn in April 1961. *Lens of Sutton Association*

Two four-car double-decker units were introduced in November 1949 on the Charing Cross-Dartford line in an experiment to increase the capacity of rush-hour services without lengthening trains or platforms. Inspired by similar units in Europe and the USA, they were designed by O.V.S. Bulleid who, with his characteristic ingenuity managed, by inter-leaving high- and low-level compartments, to pack 508 ordinary seats and 44 tip-up seats into each set, which compared to 386 seats in a standard '4-SUB'. Unfortunately, the double-decker concept quickly proved unsuitable for the more restricted British loading gauge and the Southern Region's passengers soon began to complain about the train, in particular the excessive heat in the upper compartments during warm weather. In addition, operationally it was found that loading and unloading was slower than on a conventional train, and with a cost around fifty per cent higher than conventional stock, no more double-deckers were built and the Southern Region was forced to resort to the costly alternative of increasing standard train lengths from eight to ten coaches. The units normally worked as a pair and were not able to run in multiple with any other SR/BR EMUs. In this picture, taken at London Bridge on 4th February 1954, set No. 4001 is nearest the camera. The double-deckers lasted until October 1971 and two of the coaches were saved for preservation.

'4-SUB' No. 4323 at London Bridge Platform 6 on a code 'L' service from Dartford via Sidcup in October 1956; the tail lamp shows that this is an Up train and the headcode should have been removed at Dartford. This set had been converted in 1945 from a three-car 1925-built '1285' Class unit with a new steel panelled trailer, the second vehicle in the set, which is of a noticeably different profile to the other three.

No. 30806 *Sir Galleron* at London Bridge with the 5.40pm Cannon Street to Dover Priory service draws admiring glances on 28th June 1956. The highest numbered 'King Arthur' was kept in immaculate condition for Hither Green's only passenger turn. It was shedded there from February 1951 until June 1959, when it moved to Eastleigh. *Sir Galleron* had been in lined green livery since November 1950 and had a flat sided 3,500 gallon tender, which was replaced with a bogie tender several months before it left for the Western section.

CHAPTER 1 - SOUTH EASTERN & CHATHAM RAILWAY STATIONS

Rebuilt 'West Country' No. 34004 *Yeovil* passes through Platform 1 with the 12.45pm Saturdays Only Cannon Street to Ramsgate on 30th May 1959. The headcode shows it will be routed over the Dartford Loop line (via Sidcup) to Dartford, then via Gravesend, Strood and Chatham which, as mentioned previously, was due to re-signalling in the Chislehurst area in connection with the North Kent 1959 main line electrification scheme. The '4-EPB' in Platform 3 is on a Charing Cross to Bromley North service.

The 'U1' Class 2-6-0s resulted from the rebuilding of the 'K1' Class 2-6-4T No. A890 *River Frome* after all of the 'River' Class 2-6-4Ts were taken out of service following a series of derailments, which culminated in a serious accident at Sevenoaks in 1927. This was the only 3-cylinder 'River' and the rebuilt engine proved successful in service, resulting in twenty similar engines being constructed at Eastleigh in 1931. No. 31898 was photographed in London Bridge Platform 10 on 30th January 1960. It was at Stewarts Lane from May 1955 until May 1961, when it was transferred to Salisbury. The headcode is unusual with lamps rather than discs and it is indicating a Victoria to Brighton via Eridge service rather than London Bridge to Brighton. The explanation may be that it would be dark before the journey was completed and that this is a weekend diversion with the wrong headcode.

The Railway Correspondence & Travel Society (RC&TS) Sussex & Kent Branch ran 'The Sussex Special Rail Tour' on 7th October 1962. 'Schools' No. 30925 *Cheltenham* took the train from London Bridge via East Croydon, Redhill, Three Bridges and Haywards Heath to Brighton, where it handed over to an LB&SCR 'Terrier' and 'E6' combination; the tour returned to London behind LB&SCR 'K' Class 2-6-0 No. 32353. *Cheltenham* was only ten weeks away from withdrawal but was the class member earmarked for preservation in the National Collection. It is currently in service on the Mid-Hants Railway, on long-term loan from the National Railway Museum. A drawing of the engine appeared on the cover of the RC&TS *Railway Observer* monthly magazine from 1936 until December 1972, the engine having been chosen because the society was founded in Cheltenham in 1928. No. 30925 had been fitted with a speedometer and AWS in January 1960; the conduit for the latter shows up clearly on the buffer beam and along the platform angle.

No. 80154 was the last of the BR Standard Class '4' 2-6-4Ts built, emerging from Brighton Works in March 1957 and allocated to Brighton shed until June 1963, when it moved to Feltham. It was transferred to Nine Elms in November 1964 and withdrawn in April 1967. No. 80154 is waiting to depart from London Bridge with the Southern Counties Touring Society 'The Four Counties Special' on 9th October 1966. It worked the train only as far as Wimbledon, 'Battle of Britain' No. 34052 *Lord Dowding* taking over for the run to Salisbury, with 'Merchant Navy' No. 35023 *Holland-Afrika Line* subsequently returning the tour to Victoria.

A typical rush-hour scene at London Bridge, as '2-HAP' No. 6047 runs into Platform 7 on 3rd August 1972, with another five EMUs in the picture. Code '16' indicated a Charing Cross to Sevenoaks via Parks Bridge and Orpington service. The black inverted triangle on the '2-HAP' signified the end of the unit containing the luggage compartment, to allow easy identification by station staff who had parcels to load or collect. The signal box and water tower are still in place.

The eleven parallel tracks of the approach lines disappear into the distance behind '4-EPB' No. 5212 as it arrives at London Bridge. Headcode '67' was for a Cannon Street to Blackheath/Slade Green via Erith service. To the left of the train is the office of David Lloyd Pigott & Co. who were one of the most important tea and coffee merchants for over 200 years, established in 1760.

Hastings DEMU No. 1018 after arrival at London Bridge in the early 1970s. This was one of the second batch of units built on the standard BR Mark 1 63ft 6in long underframes and was designated Class '202' under TOPS. The blue and grey livery was introduced from September 1967 and was a great improvement over the plain blue scheme. The tower block in the background is not the fifteen-storey building constructed as part of 'Operation London Bridge', which was not completed until 1975.

Two '4-EPB' units, No. 5018 with No. 5035 behind, stand in the 'Brighton' terminal platforms in the early 1970s. On the right, another '4-EPB' is in the 'Chatham' Platform 11.

2 – Bricklayers Arms

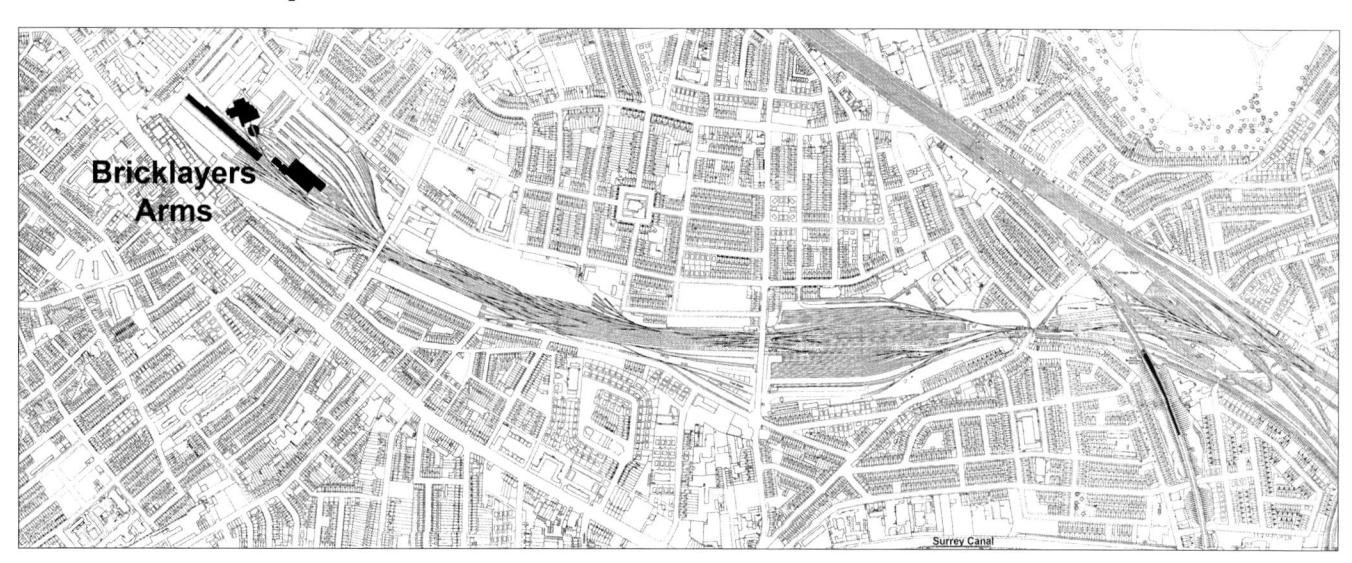

The London & Croydon Railway (later absorbed into the LB&SCR) and South Eastern Railway opened a station at Bricklayers Arms in 1844, ostensibly as a 'West End' terminus, in a tactical move to force the London & Greenwich Railway to reduce the toll it charged on trains using its London Bridge station. The terminus was at the end of a 1¾ mile branch from the L&CR's line and was on a site of around 26 acres. The opening of the station quickly had the desired effect on the tariff, with the L&CR reverting to London Bridge in March 1845; the SER used the terminus until 1852. The train shed became a goods depot and a new 5-acre goods depot was built at Willow Walk on the north side of the branch; the engine shed continued in use by the SER. Access was difficult, since the spur to the shed faced 'away' from the London stations. Engines going to Cannon Street or Charing Cross left along the branch past the Central section sidings, uphill to North Kent signal box and the main line, before reversing for the run through the heavily utilised lines to London Bridge.

As the map shows, the shed built on the site was located within one of the largest goods depots on the former Southern Railway and hence a large proportion of its work was on freight duties. It was modernised in the 1930s, when a large repair depot with wheel drop and overhead cranes was constructed in 1934. In 1936, the 'old' shed was rebuilt with a steel and asbestos roof, and a water softener and larger 65-foot turntable were installed. The depot suffered extensive damage in the war and it declined in the late-1950s as dieselisation and the Kent Coast electrification took hold. In the 1930s and 1940s, it had a large allocation of 4-4-0 types of classes 'E', 'L', 'L1' and 'Schools', over twenty 2-6-0s and a plethora of tank engines. In May 1951, three LM&SR-designed Fairburn 2-6-4Ts were transferred from Stewarts Lane, followed soon after by six Ivatt 2-6-2Ts and then another three 2-6-4Ts. In 1957-58, ten rebuilt 'Light Pacifics' arrrived, followed in 1959 by another eight (three of which were the return of earlier transfers which had only stayed for a few months) plus one unrebuilt engine, giving a total of sixteen by June 1959. By 1960, only a handful of main line duties remained, worked by its Bulleid 'Pacifics' and 'N' Class 2-6-0s, and the shed closed in 1962.

1950s

'Schools' 4-4-0 No. 30901 *Winchester* at Bricklayers Arms on 15th April 1954. During this period, more than twenty 'Schools' were based at the shed for mixed duties on the South Eastern and Central Sections and were used daily on the Charing Cross/Cannon Street/London Bridge to Folkestone/Dover/Deal/Walmer/Margate trains and Hastings which would normally consist of anything between six and eleven coaches. No. 30901 was one of the early 1948 repaints into British Railways lined black livery, with the lining on the cab extended to just below the window, and originally with BRITISH RAILWAYS in full on the tender. This has been replaced by a small version of the first emblem positioned in line with the cab numbers, rather than centrally between the horizontal lining. *Winchester* was fitted with a Lemaître multiple jet exhaust in 1940. It also has the lower type of cab window and cut-out, which were increased in height by around six inches from No. 30910 onwards.

No. 30804 *Sir Cador of Cornwall*, one of the Eastern section 'King Arthurs' with a six-wheeled 3,500 gallon tender. This picture was taken at Bricklayers Arms soon after its transfer from Ashford to Dover in June 1957. No. 30804 had recently received a General Overhaul, completed in April, during which its tender acquired the later British Railways crest. It is standing in front of the 'old' shed which had been rebuilt in 1936 with a steel and asbestos roof.

Ex-LB&SCR 'E3' 0-6-2T No. 32461 at Bricklayers Arms in February 1957, just two months before it was withdrawn. It was built as LB&SCR No. 461 in December 1895 and named *Staplefield* in the tradition of that railway. The first 'E3' was originally classified as an 'E Class Special' and was designed by William Stroudley but not finished until after his untimely death in December 1889; it was the forerunner of 134 0-6-2 radial tanks built for the LB&SCR. Although designed as a goods engine, the class were frequently used on passenger services which led to R.J. Billinton producing the 'E4', an almost identical locomotive but with 5ft diameter driving wheels, 6ins larger than those of the 'E3'.

Billinton's 'E6' 0-6-2 radial tank was introduced the month after his death in November 1904 and was very similar to his 'E5' Class. They differed in having the steam chest under the cylinders, which were increased in diameter from $17^1/_2$ins to 18ins and were also fitted with outside brake rods. No. 32418, pictured on 4th June 1959, had been transferred to Bricklayers Arms from Norwood Junction in July 1959; it stayed until January 1961, when it moved to Feltham.

1960s

The 'E4' 0-6-2T was the most common of the LB&SCR radial 0-6-2Ts, numbering seventy-five examples, of which were four were rebuilt as 'E4X'. No. 32565, originally named *Littleton*, worked trials from Battersea as an oil burner in 1902-03, using Bell & Holden's injector system, on semi-fasts to Tunbridge Wells. No. 32565 was sent to France (ROD) in November 1917, returning to England in 1919 and later becoming the first 'E4' to receive BR lined black livery, at Ashford in November 1948. It was allocated to Bricklayers Arms throughout its BR days, until withdrawn in June 1961. Also in the photograph are two 2-6-4Ts built in the 1950s; BR 'Standard' No. 80014 was at Tunbridge Wells West from 1951 until 1963, while Fairburn No. 42071 was a Three Bridges engine from November 1956 until December 1959.

Bricklayers Arms received six new Ivatt Class '2' 2-6-2Ts in 1951, including No. 41300, photographed there on 20th June 1960. They were used on Holborn Viaduct, London Bridge and Wandsworth Road shunts, Southwark Depot trips and ECS work, and also a banking duty up to Forest Hill. Built at Crewe in March 1952, No. 41300 stayed at Bricklayers Arms until early 1961, moving away to Brighton when the Ivatts were replaced by BR 'Standard' Class '2' 2-6-2Ts.

A late survivor of the SE&CR Wainwright 'C' Class 0-6-0s, complete with overhead line warning flashes, No. 31268 poses at Bricklayers Arms, probably in early 1961. It was built in 1904 at Ashford and was part of the clear out of South Eastern steam to Nine Elms in June 1959. No. 31268 moved on to Hither Green in February 1960 and then Ashford in May 1961; it was withdrawn in May 1962. The 'C' Class were 'maids of all work' and could be found on Waddon Marsh trips, New Cross Gate shunts and trips, and turns to Catford Bridge, Bromley South and Beckenham. They even worked passenger trains such as the Hop Pickers specials and other summer excursions to Kent.

No. 31719 was a 'C' Class 0-6-0 built by Sharp, Stewart in 1901 and had been at Bricklayers Arms since December 1961, after it was transferred there from Stewarts Lane. It was withdrawn within three weeks of this picture being taken on 28th April 1962.

A wintry scene in early 1963, with the water softening plant installed in the 1930s in the background. 'C' Class 0-6-0 No. 31271 had moved to Bricklayers Arms from Nine Elms in November 1961 and was withdrawn from there in July 1963. It was transferred to Departmental Stock and moved to Ashford Works, where it was initially a works shunter and then served as a stationary boiler until late 1967. BR 'Standard' 2-6-4T No. 80140 was at Tunbridge Wells West from the end of 1959 until September 1963, when it was transferred to Brighton.

No. DS1197, a 36-ton relieving-bogie breakdown crane built for the Southern Railway as No. 1197S in 1937, was based at Bricklayers Arms. The crane is standing in its shelter in front of the 'St Patrick's Shed', which was the nickname bestowed on the engine repair shed. This was a former carriage shed and was not well suited to locomotive work but, after suffering fire damage, was rebuilt in the 1930s as part of the modernisation of the shed.

3 – Holborn Viaduct to Loughborough Junction

The London Chatham & Dover Railway line from Holborn Viaduct and Blackfriars ran to Loughborough Junction, where it passed under the South London Line and the LC&DR Catford Loop before continuing to Herne Hill. In addition to the suburban and main line services, it carried cross-London freight to Herne Hill sorting sidings from the northern lines via the tunnel from Farringdon and Elephant & Castle. Traffic to Hither Green went from Blackfriars to London Bridge via Metropolitan Junction or onto the Catford Loop line, turning left just before Loughborough Junction station and then via Nunhead and Lewisham.

Elephant & Castle

Stratford's North British Locomotive Company Type '1' diesels were used on cross-London freight work during their short working lives of less than ten years. The ten Bo-Bo diesel electrics were based on the LM&SR/NBL prototype No. 10800 and had a 800bhp Paxman engine which proved unreliable in service. No. D8407 entered traffic in September 1958 and was the last of the class in service, going into store in early 1968 before its formal withdrawal in September of that year. Here, it passes through Elephant & Castle station en route to Hither Green on 19th April 1961. It would have travelled from the Eastern Region through the tunnel from Farringdon, emerging at Holborn Viaduct, and will leave the former SE&CR line at Loughborough Junction, going onto the four-track section built for the use of the two companies by the LB&SCR through Denmark Hill, before re-joining the SE&CR line at Peckham Rye and Nunhead. No. D8407 is displaying one of the special cross-London inter-regional headcodes, the three discs indicating a train working between the Eastern Region and Hither Green sidings. Elephant & Castle station had new canopies following bomb damage in the war.

Loughborough Junction

'O1' 0-6-0 No. 31048 with a northbound freight at Loughborough Junction on 25th May 1959. The train is passing under the bridge carrying the South London and Catford Loop lines over the Herne Hill-Blackfriars main line at the south end of the station. The 'O1' was an SE&CR Wainwright rebuild of the SER Stirling 'O' Class 0-6-0, with a domed boiler and a squared cab replacing the original domeless boiler and round-top cab. No. 31048 had been built at Ashford in 1893 and was rebuilt as an 'O1' in 1908. It was allocated to Stewarts Lane until June 1959 when it was part of the mass clear-out of steam to Nine Elms, before moving to Dover Marine in February 1960 until withdrawal in October that year. Note the original narrow Stirling tender with the springs and their hangers above the footplate.

4 – South London Line

The South London Line was built by the LB&SCR and followed a crescent-shaped route through the inner suburbs of south London, from Battersea Park to London Bridge; it opened fully in 1867. Originally, the line was poorly patronised but its fortunes changed when Stroudley's 'A1X' Class 'Terrier' 0-6-0Ts with new sets of four-wheeled coaches were introduced on the service. These were replaced with Billinton 'E4' 0-6-2Ts by around 1900 but competition from the motorbus and the tram saw another decline, and after much investigation the LB&SCR decided to electrify the line using a 6,700 volt, single phase alternating current system; the electric service over the 8.6 route miles began on 1st December 1909. The line was extensively publicised, as the 'South London Elevated Electric', with a quarter-hourly interval service and journey times reduced from 36 to 24 minutes. As a result, passenger numbers rose from 3.5 million in 1903 to 12 million by 1920. Eight three-coach trains comprising two open Third Class motor coaches and a First Class trailer were built by the Metropolitan Amalgamated Carriage & Wagon Company in Birmingham. The trailers were soon found to be unnecessary and a two-car formation of a Driving trailer and Compartment First/Third Control trailers was adopted.

In 1923, the Southern Railway inherited two different electric systems and chose the L&SWR 600v dc third rail after taking expert advice from the Pennsylvania Railroad in the USA. The South London Line was converted to 600v dc on 17th June 1928, the original two-car units being converted in 1929 after about a year of operation using standard three-car sets. It was not until 1951 that some of these were replaced with Third Class only '2-NOL' units. Finally, in March 1954, new '2-EPB' units were introduced and by September of that year the rebuilt units were all withdrawn.

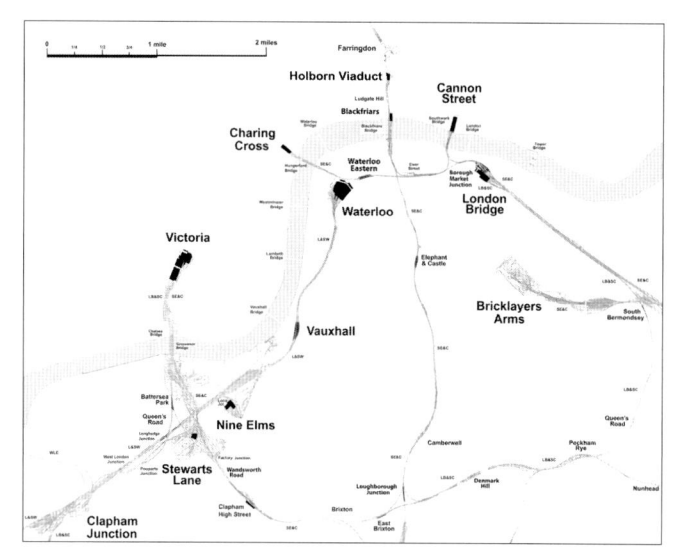

After the 1923 Grouping, the South London Line began a long period of decline and, by 1938, off-peak services had been reduced to two per hour, increased to every twenty minutes at peak times. This continued after the Second World War and the same service was maintained into the 1970s; the Sunday service was taken off in 1976 and the Saturday one in 1981, with a further reduction to a peak-hour only service in 1984. Closure was rumoured but, after public pressure, British Rail revamped the line in 1991, branding it as the 'South London Link' and restoring the mid-week half-hourly service. It continued in operation until December 2012, the intermediate stations thence being served by the 'London Overground' from Clapham Junction.

South Bermondsey

'4-SUB' No. 4346 at South Bermondsey on a service from London Bridge to Tulse Hill, Crystal Palace Low Level, Sydenham and back to London Bridge, on 9th January 1961. Trains on the service running in the opposite direction had a single dot above the 'P' in the headcode. The island platform, situated on an embankment, was opened in 1928, replacing the original South Bermondsey station which was a quarter of a mile nearer to London Bridge, the 7 miles 31 chains from which were all on a brick viaduct at roof level. In the background are the approach lines into the Bricklayers Arms yards, which the South London Line crossed here.

K.G. Carr

'2-SL' EMU No. 1806 at Queen's Road Peckham on 30th July 1954, with the leading vehicle No. S9756S, a Driving Composite trailer. Eight two-car sets were introduced in May 1929 by rebuilding and converting to dc operation the sixteen original ac South London Line Driving vehicles, formed into a Third Class Driving motor coach and a First/Third Driving trailer. Note the panelled sides and the lower roof above the driver's cab and guard's compartment, a throwback to where the ac overhead bow collector had been positioned. The coaches were 9ft 5ins wide over commode handles, which meant that the sets could not operate on most lines, where there was a width restriction of 9ft 0in, which probably contributed to their longevity on the South London Line.
The Lens of Sutton Association

No. 4630, a 1949-built '4-SUB' seen here at Queen's Road Peckham, was one of the first sets produced with three open and one compartment vehicle instead of the fully compartment stock previously built. A single island platform replaced the separate Up and Down platforms of the original Queen's Road station; it was built where a third track in the centre had once been, up until 1933.

Peckham Rye

A '2-EPB', No. 5222, on a South London line train from Victoria to London Bridge approaches the junction at Peckham Rye, with the line to Tulse Hill diverging to the left, on 17th February 1957. In the background with the two arched roofs is the original LB&SCR electric maintenance depot where the South London line sets were based. In front is a later addition. The maintenance sheds closed in around 1965 with the work being transferred to Selhurst depot. Berthing of units lasted until April 1967 and the site was flattened in 1969.
R.C. Riley/The Transport Treasury

Peckham Rye still has wooden platforms as rebuilding work is in progress on 18th January 1961. As at Queen's Road, an island platform was constructed on the former trackbed before the two separate platforms were removed. No. 4346, on a London Bridge to London Bridge service via Tulse Hill, Crystal Palace Low Level and Sydenham, was an augmented '4-SUB' formed from '3-SUB' No. 1516 with the addition of a steel intermediate trailer; it ran until December 1961.
K.G. Carr

Wandsworth Road

'2-SL' unit No. 1808, with Motor Brake Third No. S8730S at the front, arrives at Wandsworth Road from Battersea Park on 19th September 1954; there was a distance of only 56 chains between the two stations. The South London Line was joined at Wandsworth Road by the former LC&DR line from Victoria, which is just visible at the end of the rear coach, and the two lines ran in parallel as far as Peckham Rye. From Wandsworth Road to East Brixton the tracks were built and owned by the LB&SCR, and vice versa from there to Peckham Rye. Each company had the exclusive use of one pair of lines but each had to maintain the other's track over the section it had built. In the centre background is the 285ft high Battersea Park No. 7 MAN-designed gas holder.
R.C. Riley/The Transport Treasury

Battersea Park

Battersea Park station looking south in the late 1940s, showing the South London Line tracks curving away to the left. The smoke is still drifting across the platforms after a train has passed through on the LB&SCR main line towards Clapham Junction. Battersea Park Junction signal box spanning this line was opened in 1906 and was in operation until 1979. The station was opened in 1867 as York Road but was renamed Battersea Park three years later.
The Lens of Sutton Association

The first of the '2-EPB' units, No. 5701, arriving at Battersea Park on the 1.17pm Victoria-London Bridge on 1st March 1954. The line was carried on a brick viaduct over Queen's Road Battersea station and the yards at Stewarts Lane. Only one mile and 20 chains from Victoria, the South London Line diverged from the LB&SCR Victoria-Brighton main line immediately before the station. In the background, painted light blue, is the lower part of the 285ft high Battersea No. 7 gas holder, which was demolished in 2015 to make way for new homes, shops and business space. *The Lens of Sutton Association*

5 – Victoria

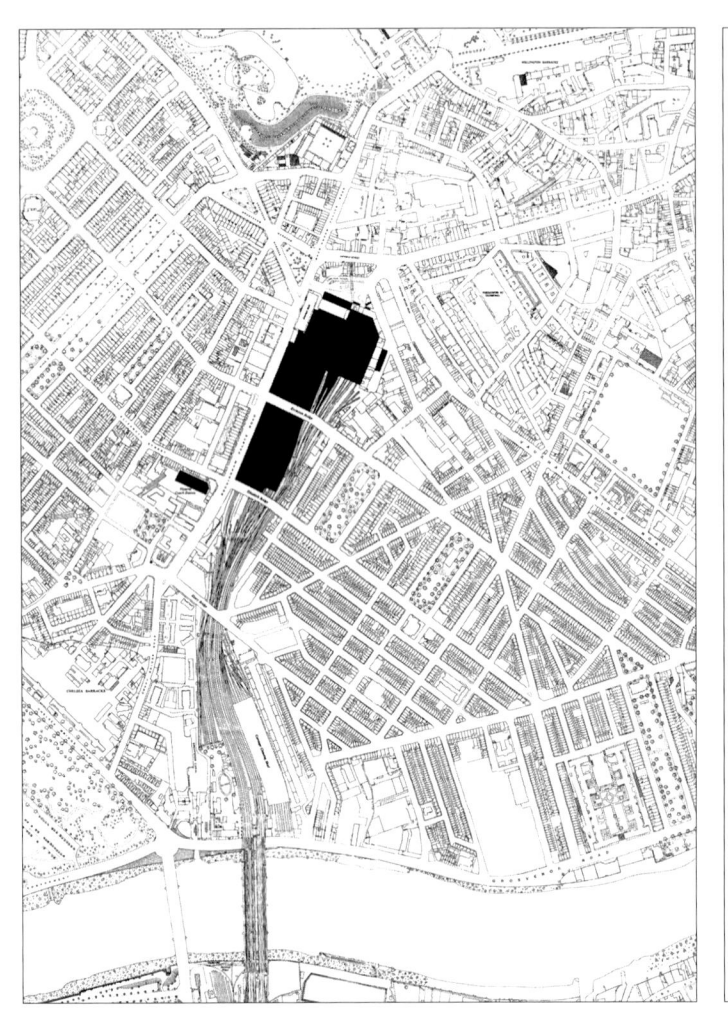

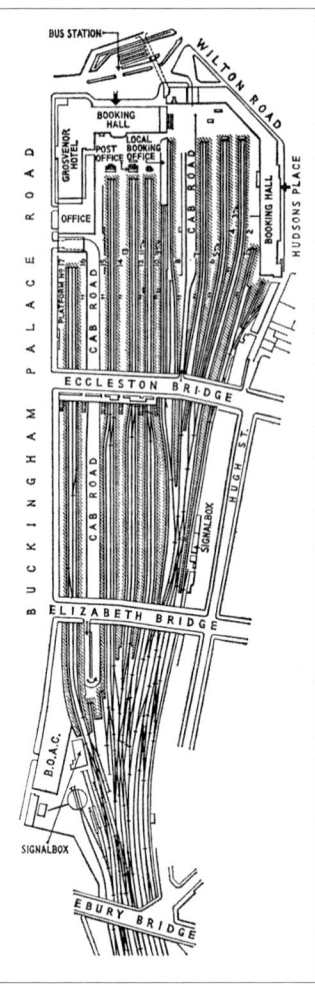

For many years, Victoria was two separate stations with the 'Central' or 'Brighton' side operating independently from the 'Eastern' side. The LB&SCR opened its West End terminus at Victoria in 1860, having reached the City at London Bridge in 1842. A temporary terminus had been opened at Pimlico in 1858 but a true West End station would be opened within two years, situated near Belgravia and only a few hundred yards from Buckingham Palace. The LB&SCR terminus took up $8^1/_2$ of the 14 acres, with the remainder of the site leased jointly by the LC&DR, formerly the East Kent Railway until 1859, and the Great Western Railway, and opening in 1862. The LC&DR had running powers into the new station from Beckenham but soon obtained powers to construct its own line into Victoria, from Beckenham to Stewarts Lane.

Over the next three decades, improvements were made to the approach roads, and the LB&SCR side of the station was completely rebuilt between 1906 and 1908, almost doubling the area occupied. Sideways expansion was not possible and so the unusual solution was adopted of increasing the length instead, effectively creating two stations end-to-end by extending the platforms between Eccleston Bridge and Elizabeth Bridge. It had nine platforms, of which eight had crossovers placed to allow two trains to use them at the same time. Five platforms were electrified in 1909 on the LB&SCR 6,600 volt ac overhead system; these were converted to 660 volt dc third rail operation in 1928-29.

The SE&CR followed suit and began demolition of its wooden frontage in 1907, replacing it a year later with a stylish French-inspired, four-storey, stone-faced building, with a central archway for the cab road and refreshment rooms managed by J. Lyons & Co. on either side. However, behind this, the ten platform faces (later reduced to eight) and the double arch roof were left virtually unchanged. The GWR trains to Southall ran until 1915.

After the 1923 Grouping, steps were taken to integrate the two stations, an opening being created in the dividing wall and improvements made to the concourse on the 'Chatham' side. The number of platform faces was reduced and in September 1925 the platforms on both sides were renumbered in a continuous sequence, from 1 to 17. In 1925, the first regular third rail service began, to Herne Hill and Orpington, with main line services to Brighton and Worthing in 1933, to Eastbourne and Hastings in 1935, and to Littlehampton, Bognor and Portsmouth via Horsham in 1938. Following electrification, the number of rush-hour passengers almost doubled between 1927 and 1937, from 10,200 to 17,200.

Victoria also handled the glamorous Continental services and improved customs facilities were provided in 1930. A new Continental inquiry, reservation and ticket office was opened in 1948, and improvements were made to the Eastern section booking hall in the 1951. Platforms 7 and 8 were extended in 1960 to accommodate the new fourteen-car electric boat trains made up of three four-car units plus one or two Motor Luggage Vans, and Platforms 1 to 6 were also lengthened; Platforms 7 and 8 had to be narrowed at the country end to help provide sufficient width for the other extensions. An unusual development was the opening of London's first rail-air terminal in 1962, in a steel and glass building above Platforms 15 and 16, for British United Airways whose flights used Gatwick airport.

Taken at 10.39am, the concourse is quite busy and there is a queue waiting at Platform 14. The large mechanical train departure board was divided into sections for each of the main routes; this one was for Central section trains with the other 'main' Eastern Section departure board to the left of this between Platforms 4 and 5. W. H. Smith is the only company featuring in the photograph which is still operating; Woolworths went into administration in 2008 and Eagle Star Insurance was taken over in 1984 and is now owned by Zurich Financial Services which no longer uses the brand.

A very quiet Victoria in the 1950s, outside the rush-hour at 10.45 in the morning, showing the entrance to the 'Golden Arrow' on the right. The manually operated departure board on the left was headed 'The Gateway to the Continent – Departure Times of the International European Expresses'.

1950s steam

No. 32424 *Beachy Head* leaves Victoria on 5th October 1952, with the RC&TS 'Brighton Works Centenary' special comprising eight Pullman cars. It covered the journey in 58.4 minutes (net 54.45), compared with a schedule of 60 minutes. After arrival at Brighton there were visits to the works and the running shed, and on each day three special trains, all hauled by 'A1X' Class 'Terrier' No. 32636, ran from Brighton to Kemp Town and back. The tour was repeated two weeks later, this time using No. 32425 *Trevose Head*. *Beachy Head* was a LB&SCR 'H2' Class 4-4-2 designed by D.E. Marsh, a superheated version of his first 'Atlantic', the 'H1'. Both classes were markedly similar to the Great Northern Railway Ivatt 'Atlantics' built at Doncaster, where Marsh had been closely involved in their design. The five 'H1' and six 'H2' 4-4-2s were all given names of well-known geographical headlands in LB&SCR territory. No. 32424 was built in September 1911 and withdrawn in April 1958. Victoria Central signal box, which was commissioned in 1939 when the station was re-signalled with colour lights, lasted until 1980, when its work was taken over by a new box at Clapham Junction, is dwarfed by the British Overseas Airways Corporation (BOAC) building. Also opened in 1939, and known as the Empire Terminal, it was used mainly by passengers who went by bus to Heathrow. The airline vacated it at the end of the 1970s; it was listed as Grade II by English Heritage in 1981 and is now occupied by the National Audit Office.

'Battle of Britain' No. 34066 *Spitfire*, here adorned with a slightly lopsided 'Kentish Belle' headboard, was at Stewarts Lane from December 1949 until February 1961. The engine was not rebuilt and was withdrawn in September 1966. The all-Pullman summer only service ran to Ramsgate via Chatham in the mid-1950s; originally titled the 'Thanet Belle' when it started in 1948, the service lasted until 1958. The train left Victoria at 11.35am, except on Saturdays when it departed at 7.55am, the journey taking slightly over two hours.

The ex-LB&SCR 'Atlantics' were used regularly on rail tours in the 1950s. No. 32425 *Trevose Head* starts the Stephenson Locomotive Society 'Portsmouth Special' on 3rd May 1953, taking nine coaches from Victoria via Pulborough, Chichester and Havant to Portsmouth & Southsea. The locomotive was built in December 1911 and was taken out of service in September 1956. The return trip to Waterloo was hauled by ex-L&SWR 'T9' No. 30718 from Portsmouth & Southsea via Petersfield, Guildford and Woking. The BOAC building in the background was extended in 1963 with an eight-storey block over the ends of Platforms 15 to 17.

'Battle of Britain' No. 34078 *222 Squadron* pulls out of Victoria with a Ramsgate train, past the Bishop & Sons furniture depository on 7th June 1956. It was allocated to Ramsgate from new in July 1948, and was transferred to Bricklayers Arms in June 1959, the only unrebuilt 'Pacific' allocated there. Platforms 1 and 2 at Victoria were not electrified until the 1959 Kent Coast phase 1 electrification.

No. 41296 on ECS duties at Victoria on 7th June 1956. Built at Crewe in October 1951, it was one of eight Ivatt Class '2' 2-6-2Ts, No's 41290-97, which went new to Stewarts Lane. It was in its third spell at the shed, having been at Three Bridges and Exmouth Junction each for about six months but would move away permanently to Barnstaple Junction in October 1956.

BR 'Standard' Class '5' 4-6-0 No. 73085 arriving at Victoria from Ramsgate, also on 7th June 1956. It was built in August 1955 and, except for a two-month spell at Oxford in early 1956, was allocated to Stewarts Lane until May 1959, when the first stage of the Kent Coast electrification began operation and it moved with eight classmates to Nine Elms. No. 73085 was named *Melisande*, taking the name from withdrawn 'King Arthur' No. 30753 in August 1959, and was itself taken out of service at the end of Southern steam in July 1967.

Wainwright 'C' Class 0-6-0 No. 31576 banking a boat train out of Platform 7 in June 1957 and providing assistance up the 1 in 64 ahead of the train. It was normal operating procedure for the engine which had brought in the empty stock to bank heavy trains out of the station. No. 31576 would move from Stewarts Lane to Gillingham three months after this picture was taken.

No. 34078 *222 Squadron* again, bankoing a boat train out of Victoria in the late 1950s; the last vehicle in the train is the usual parcels van. There is a lot of preparatory work going on in connection with the platform extension work for the first phase of the Kent Coast Electrification. Note also the 'modern' canopy recently erected on Platforms 1 and 2. Behind the engine is Victoria Eastern signal box, built in 1920 as Victoria 'A' and renamed in 1939 when colour light signalling was introduced, which controlled the former SE&CR lines. The large building in the centre background belonged to the Bishop & Sons removals company, which was established in 1854 and is now the largest privately-owned removals business in the UK, with over twenty branches across the country and in Europe, operating under the name 'Bishop's Move'.

CHAPTER 5 - VICTORIA

In a picture taken from above the throat of Grosvenor Road carriage sidings/shed on the South Eastern side of Victoria at the foot of Grosvenor Bank, 'D1' 4-4-0 No. 31749 approaches the station on 28th July 1956, probably with an ECS working given the driver's posture. Ebury Bridge housing estate is in the background, as is the small signal box controlling the Up side carriage and parcels sidings alongside the Grosvenor Canal. No. 31749 was at Stewarts Lane until transferred to Bricklayers Arms in June 1959, avoiding the mass exodus to Nine Elms and staying until withdrawn in November 1961.

'West Country' Class No. 34098 *Templecombe* outside Victoria carriage shed facing towards the station on 6th May 1956. Built in December 1949 at Brighton, it went to Ramsgate until February 1958, when it was transferred to Bournemouth.

One of the 'Scotch Arthurs', No. 30776 *Sir Galagars*, runs in under Elizabeth Bridge in the 1950s. Built by the North British Locomotive Company in June 1925, it was originally allocated to Nine Elms, hence the 5,000 gallon bogie tender. No. 30776 moved to the Eastern section at Stewarts Lane in April 1945 and then on to Dover from February 1951 until withdrawn in January 1959.

Two batches of the SE&CR Wainwright 'C' Class 0-6-0s were built by outside contractors, including No. 31690, which came from Neilsons of Glasgow in 1900. Having brought in the empty stock, No. 31690 is assisting the train engine with the 1 in 64 climb to Grosvenor Bridge on 13th April 1958. It was allocated to Hither Green, leaving there in November 1961 for Chart Leacon at Ashford.

'Golden Arrow'

In 1924, shortly after the formation of the Southern Railway, an all-Pullman relief to the 11.00 am Dover boat train was introduced, with a corresponding train running in the opposite direction. The Southern built a First Class only ferry, the *Canterbury*, especially for the service. Across the Channel, it connected with the SNCF Calais-Paris Pullman and from the summer of 1929 was given the name 'Golden Arrow', the French train having been christened the 'Flèche d'Or' in 1926. The popularity of the train declined in the late 1930s and the original ten First Class Pullmans had reduced to four, including Second Class accommodation, but it was relaunched, accompanied by considerable publicity, in 1946. After being displayed at the 1951 Festival of Britain, 'Britannia' No. 70004 *William Shakespeare* went to Stewarts Lane along with No. 70014 *Iron Duke* to work the 'Golden Arrow' service and other boat trains to Dover and Folkestone. Both engines were kept in immaculate condition, as demonstrated here by No. 70004 waiting at Platform 8 with the 'Golden Arrow' in around 1955. The 'Britannia' is adorned with a large headboard on the smokebox, arrows on the smoke deflectors and the British and French flags on the front footplate.

No. 70014 *Iron Duke*, waiting at Victoria on 24th March 1956, was allocated to Nine Elms for its first three months on the Southern Region, moving to Stewarts Lane in September 1951. It was usually the reserve engine to No. 70004 *William Shakespeare* for the 'Golden Arrow'. Both engines were at Stewarts Lane until June 1958 when they were transferred to the London Midland Region, and the 'Golden Arrow' reverted to Bulleid 'Pacifics' for its final years of steam haulage. As well as significantly raising the height of the lamp irons on both of these 'Britannias', the Southern Region also moved the other lamp brackets from the front platform up to the lower angle irons on the smokebox sides supporting the smoke deflectors.

'Battle of Britain' No. 34086 *219 Squadron* storms out of Victoria under the Elizabeth Bridge with the 'Golden Arrow'. The arrows fixed to the side casings on the Bulleid engines were massive and much longer than those provided for the 'Britannias', which had to fit on the smoke deflectors. When built at Brighton in December 1948, No. 34086 was painted in experimental apple green livery but this was replaced by standard green in October 1950. It was at Ramsgate until October 1957, moving to Exmouth Junction before returning to the Eastern section at Dover in February 1958 and Stewarts Lane a month later.

CHAPTER 5 - VICTORIA

Blue-liveried No. E5004 at Victoria prior to departure with the 'Golden Arrow' in September 1967. By this date, the number of Pullman coaches in the train had been reduced and ordinary stock substituted. The electric had entered traffic in April 1959 and became No. 71004 in 1974. It was stored, theoretically serviceable, at Hither Green in October 1976 and withdrawn a year later. The first electric-hauled 'Arrow' was on 12th June 1961. When the rail blue era arrived, the Pullmans lost their distinctive livery in favour of the new BR blue and grey, although the British and French flags were still displayed on the locomotive but the arrows on the bodyside had been dispensed with. The Pullmans were all repainted by 1969, by which date the cars were no longer known by their names, simply by their stock numbers. The final 'Golden Arrow' ran on 30th September 1972.

'Night Ferry'

'Battle of Britain' No. 34073 249 Squadron and a classmate after arrival at Victoria on the 'Night Ferry' in 1953. The 'Night Ferry', consisting of Compagnie Internationale des Wagon-Lits sleeping cars, was introduced in 1936 as a response to the embryonic airline competition. Arrangements were made with CIWL to run a through service of sleeping cars from London to Paris and European pattern vehicles were built to fit within the Southern Railway loading gauge. The train was withdrawn in 1939 but reinstated at the end of 1947 and ran until October 1980. The journey time from London to Paris was approximately twelve hours. In summer 1953, the train left Paris Gare du Nord at 9.45pm and was booked to reach Victoria at 9.10am, although delays were commonplace, often due to difficulties with the ferry crossing. The time is 10.55am so it looks as if the train is ready to be backed out of the terminus. In the other direction, departure from Victoria was at 10pm and arrival at Gare du Nord was at 9am. Passengers had to be at Victoria 'not later than thirty minutes before the advertised departure in order to comply with HM Customs and Immigration formalities'. The use of two Bulleid 'Pacifics' would not be commonplace, so perhaps the train was unusually heavy on this day. No. 34073 was the third 'Light Pacific' built with a 9ft wide, wedge-shaped cab with three windows. Constructed at Brighton in May 1948 and originally allocated to Ramsgate, it moved to Dover in January 1949, remaining there until May 1961. No. 34073 was never rebuilt and after withdrawal in June 1964 went to Woodham Brothers scrapyard in South Wales. It left there in 1988 for the proposed Brighton Railway Museum project and when that foundered it was stored at Ropley on the Mid-Hants Railway. It has still not been restored, the last unrebuilt 'Light Pacific' not yet returned to traffic and is currently at the West Coast Railway Centre in Carnforth, awaiting a decision on its future but in the meantime having donated parts to keep No. 34067 Tangmere operational.

CHAPTER 5 - VICTORIA

No. E5007 brings in the 'Night Ferry' stock to Victoria in the early 1960s, just over half an hour before departure. The train is in Platform 2, which was extended in 1960 to take eighteen vehicles. No. E5007 is here still in its original livery, with a horizontal red stripe along the body and no yellow warning panel. It was built at Doncaster in June 1959, renumbered as No. 71007 in 1974 and taken out of traffic in August 1976, although not formally withdrawn until November 1977.

No. E5017 after arrival at Victoria with the 'Night Ferry' in 1961; the headboard was in the same style as that used for the 'Golden Arrow'. The locomotive entered traffic in April 1960. It was taken out of service for conversion at Crewe Works to an electro-diesel in April 1967, becoming No. E6109 in April 1968 when it returned to traffic and then No. 74009 in 1974; the conversions were not successful and it was withdrawn at the end of 1977.

Electric traction

The length of the platforms from the 1909 extension is apparent in this view. The EMU is one of the '6-PUL' sets built in 1932 for the express services to Brighton and Worthing and containing a Pullman car. Note the 'extra' track starting in front of Eccleston Bridge by the Pullman car; these allowed the Brighton platforms to each accept two eight-car trains. The middle line was introduced so that the train nearest the buffers could leave when there was one still standing behind it but the twelve-car train in the photograph is fouling the turnout for this. When the station was redeveloped in the late 1970s, the extra lines were removed and the buffer stops were moved two or three coaches towards the country end of the station to allow for a considerable enlargement of the concourse.
The Lens of Sutton Association

'2-HAL' No. 2651, built in 1939 for the Maidstone and Gillingham services, leaving on the 9.18am Victoria to Gillingham in May 1956. It is heading under Ebury Road Bridge and will shortly pass the extensive Victoria carriage shed, situated on the Down side of the line. These units had a number of new features compared with earlier stock, including steel panelled construction on hardwood frames and welded rolled steel cab ends with domed roofs. The windows were as flush as possible with the sides and they had large radius rounded corners. They were formed of a Driving Motor Brake Third and a Driving Trailer Composite.

CHAPTER 5 - VICTORIA

'2-EPB' No. 5706 on a train to London Bridge via the South London Line on 6th May 1956. Built in 1954 for the extended ten-coach trains, they were also used to replace the '2-SL' units on the South London Line.

A gathering of platform-enders chatting to the driver of No. E5007 as it waits to depart from Victoria, probably with the 'Golden Arrow', since all the boat trains except the 'Night Ferry' were twelve-car '4-CEP/BEP' formations. This was one of the Bo-Bo electric locomotives introduced in 1959 for the Kent Coast Electrification scheme and the picture was clearly taken in the mid-1960s, because No. E5007 has a small yellow warning panel and has lost its original red horizontal body stripe. It was built in June 1959 and renumbered as No. 71007 in 1974.

Passengers for the boat train walk past Motor Luggage Van No. 68009 at Platform 2 in the late 1960s. Ten of these were built in 1959-61 to provide additional luggage space on the Continental boat trains and were used for registered baggage which was customs cleared at both ends of the journey. They were built on standard length 63ft 6ins underframes and had three double doors on each side opening onto two luggage compartments, plus a compartment for bonded consignments. They were powered by two 250hp traction motors, whilst for working over the non-electrified quayside lines when baggage was loaded directly onto the ships from the quayside, current was supplied from a battery power set. No. 68009 was built in March 1961 at Eastleigh. Note the large neon 'Night Ferry' sign in the background.

No. 5018, one of the second batch of '4-EPB's built in 1953, at Platform 11 on a South London Line service to London Bridge in around 1970. The large sign halfway down the adjacent platform is for 'May & Philpot - Streatham Norbury Brixton - Surveyors Estate Agents Valuers', who are still in business today as part of HNF Property.

6 – Victoria to Brixton

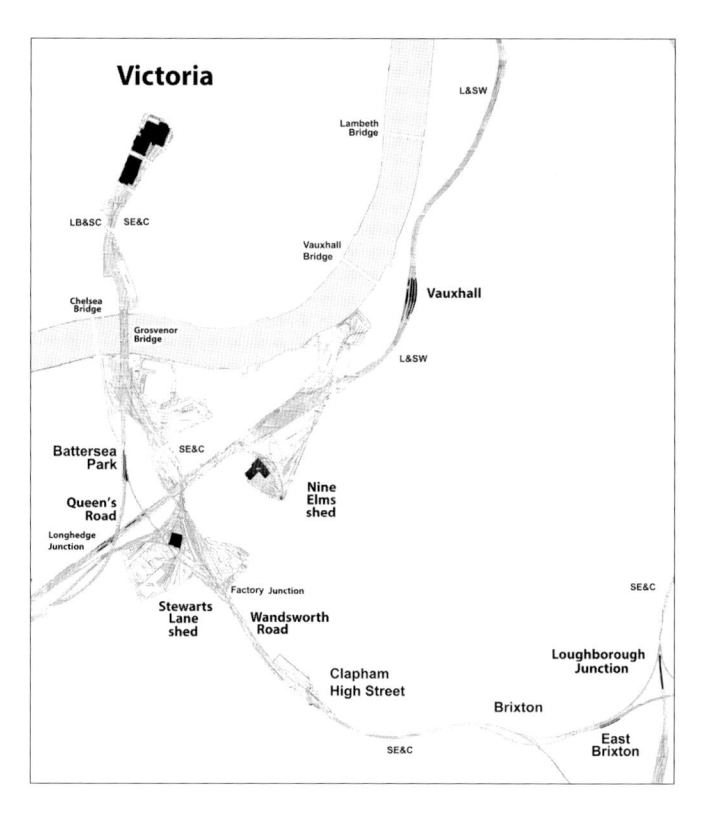

The lines from Victoria started on the north of the river, with the LB&SCR and SE&CR routes crossing to the south over Grosvenor Bridge. Its predecessor, the Victoria Bridge, was the first railway bridge to be built over the Thames, in 1860. The crossing was quickly expanded from two to seven tracks by building a new bridge alongside the old, and this was repeated in 1907 adding two more tracks on the other side of the old structure. They had all deteriorated by the 1960s and were replaced by a new ten-track bridge with separate spans for each track.

There was a station within a short distance of the terminus, at Battersea Park on the LB&SCR main line/South London Line, before the LB&SCR ran alongside the L&SWR from Longhedge Junction and carried on towards Clapham Junction. The South London Line diverged away towards Wandsworth Road, crossing over the L&SWR main line from Waterloo at Queen's Road Battersea station and then over the Stewarts Lane shed and goods depot.

The two SE&CR lines out of Victoria split after Grosvenor Bridge, passing one under and one over the L&SWR main line a short distance away, before meeting again at Factory Junction where they were joined by the South London Line. Immediately, all three routes then passed through Wandsworth Road station and the two company's lines ran in parallel as far as Peckham Rye.

From Wandsworth Road to East Brixton, the tracks were built and owned by the LC&DR, later the SE&CR, and one pair was used by the LB&SCR, and vice versa from there to Peckham Rye. Each company had the exclusive use of its 'own' lines but each had to maintain the other's track over the section it had built.

'King Arthur' No. 30797 *Sir Blamor de Ganis* climbs the 1 in 64 Grosvenor bank past the carriage shed on the Down 'Kentish Belle' to Ramsgate in 1955, on what was normally a Bulleid 'Pacific' turn. It was built at Eastleigh in June 1926 and was always paired with a 3,500 gallon six-wheeled tender. No. 30797 spent all except its first seven years on the Eastern section and had been at Dover since July 1953; it was withdrawn in May 1959.

Battersea Park

With Battersea power station in the background, two ex-GWR 'Dukedog' 4-4-0s, No's 9011 and 9023, have just departed from Victoria with the RC&TS 'Swindon & Highworth Rail Tour', which they worked on the outward journey, on 25th April 1954. A number of these engines had been stored in Swindon's stock shed for some time when they were displaced from the ex-Cambrian Railways lines in central Wales. A few weeks earlier, however, in March, No. 9023 had been used on pilot duties over the south Devon banks between Plymouth North Road and Newton Abbot but the experiment was short-lived, probably because the local enginemen did not take too favourably to an engine with such an exposed cab, open to all that the south Devon weather could throw at them!

'4-CIG' No. 7324 in its original all green livery with small yellow warning panel in the corridor connection, takes the former LB&SCR Down Local line through Battersea Park towards Clapham Junction on an ECS working to Streatham Hill sidings in around 1967; the South London Line branches off to the right. The '4-CIG' units were built between 1964 and 1966 to replace the '6-PAN' and '6-PUL' sets on the Central section. In the background, another '4-CIG' is parked on what was the Up side siding road that extended across Grosvenor Bridge to Victoria. A '4-SUB' is approaching on the Down Through line. On the right is the lower part of the gas holder seen in previous pictures. Painted light blue, it featured alongside neighbouring Battersea power station in the 1973 artwork for the *Quadrophenia* album of the rock band 'The Who'. The gas holder was designed by the German company MAN but was built in 1932 by an English company called R.&J. Dempster, who held a licence from MAN.

Stewarts Lane

The pride and joy of Stewarts Lane, No. 70004 *William Shakespeare* on the Down 'Golden Arrow', is passing its home shed which is just out of picture on the left. In the background is the familiar form of Battersea power station, the first part of which was built in the 1930s, although the second phase, which resulted in the four-chimney layout, was not built until after the war. It did not come into full operation until 1955, as shown by the chimney nearest the camera which was still under construction. The power station was closed in March 1975 and was given Grade II listed status in 1980; the building and the surrounding site is currently being redeveloped as an up-market residential location. New Pullman stock had been introduced for the 'Golden Arrow' in 1951, built by the Birmingham Railway Carriage & Wagon Co., eight First Class carriages continuing the Pullman tradition of names instead of numbers, and two Second Class carrying car numbers. The train shown consists of nine of these coaches and three vans for luggage. Note the gas wagon in the sidings on the left.

The penultimate 'Merchant Navy' to enter traffic, in February 1949, No. 35029 *Ellerman Lines* passes Stewarts Lane shed yard in the early 1950s, with Battersea power station again in the background; the fourth chimney, still under construction, was not completed until 1955. The photograph was taken after July 1952 when the front casing was removed and No. 35029 was repainted from BR blue to green. It was not rebuilt until 1959 and, after withdrawal and seven years at Barry scrapyard, was purchased by the National Railway Museum and is now a sectioned exhibit at York Railway Museum. No. 35029 is heading a Down express with an eclectic collection of stock, including Maunsell, Bulleid and BR Mark 1 coaches, two Pullman cars and two GUVs, painted in a mix of SR malachite green and BR 'blood and custard' liveries. The high level, former LC&DR route had three tracks but only two were electrified in 1925, the third being treated in 1959 as part of the Kent Coast Electrification Phase 1. The approach line into Wandsworth Road goods depot is just visible on the right.
The Lens of Sutton Association

This is the north side of Stewarts Lane shed, with the Hampton & Sons Ltd furniture depository in the background. The lower windows are bricked up, which appears to have happened between 1939 and early 1950, presumably carried out to minimise blast damage in the war. The Western Region 'Pannier' tank is probably heading for Battersea Yard to collect a transfer freight to the WR; it would be a few more years before some of them were allocated to the Southern Region. The ex-Great Northern Railway 'J52' 0-6-0T appears to have 'British Railways' in full on the tank sides below the handrail and is either No. 68758 or No. 68759, both allocated to Hornsey until September 1952 and used on transfer trips.

CHAPTER 6 - VICTORIA TO BRIXTON

Ex-SE&CR Wainwright Class 'C' 0-6-0 No. 31578 heading a short train of empty milk tanks in 1959, probably out to Clapham Junction; the train has just passed under the bridge carrying the South London line. It was allocated to Stewarts Lane throughout its British Railways career until withdrawn in June 1961. Billinton 'K' Class 2-6-0 No. 32338 from Brighton shed heads a line of engines on the right. This was the second engine of the class, built in 1913, and it was in service until the end of 1962. In the background on the right is the Stewarts Lane coaling plant and on the left, partly obscured by the smoke from No. 31578, is the Hampton's Depository.

Clapham High Street

Although the Southern Railway built the 'W' Class 2-6-4Ts for its transfer freight work, the other companies used their ordinary freight and tank engines. L&NER 'J50' 0-6-0T No. 68966, working a freight on 7th November 1960, is passing Clapham (High Street) station on the Down LC&DR line towards Brixton Junction and then will almost certainly travel via Canterbury Road Junction, Loughborough Junction, Blackfriars and the Widened Lines to King's Cross. The engine carries a cross-London inter-regional headlamp code and was allocated to Hornsey from March 1956, being withdrawn in July 1961.

'W' Class 2-6-4T No. 31922 works another cross-London freight, on the LC&DR Up Relief alongside the South London Line station at Clapham (High Street), going towards Factory Junction with a train from Hither Green to Old Oak Common, also on 7th November 1960.

The Lens of Sutton Association

Brixton

Class 'N1' 2-6-0 No. 31876 takes the line towards Brixton station and Herne Hill as it crosses the bridge over Brixton Road, with the Catford Loop diverging to the right, in June 1956. Marks & Spencer are still trading today from the building to the left of the engine but Bon Marché, to the right, closed down in June 1975. Named after the famous store in Paris, it was the first purpose-built department store and the first steel-frame building in the country when opened in 1877. The original business was bought by Selfridges in 1926, and then by the John Lewis Partnership in 1940. At the 1923 Grouping there were twelve ex-S&ECR Maunsell 'N' Class 2-cylinder locomotives in service. The thirteenth, No. A822, classified 'N1', was built in 1923 with three cylinders, the two outside with Walschaerts valve gear and the inside cylinder with Holcroft conjugated valve gear, which derived the motion for the inside valve from that of the outside valves. Externally, its appearance was very similar, with the most noticeable difference the much deeper buffer beam when compared with the 'N' Class. No. 31876 was the first of five new engines built in 1930 using Walschaerts valve gear on all three cylinders. It was allocated to Hither Green between June 1950 and June 1959; all six 'N1's were withdrawn in October/November 1962.

7 – Stewarts Lane

Stewarts Lane shed was right in the middle of the incredible complex of lines leaving Victoria; the LC&DR Ludgate Hill Branch and the LB&SCR South London Line ran virtually over the rear of the shed, the high- and low-level LC&DR lines passed to one side and the LB&SCR route towards Clapham Junction on the other. The former Longhedge Works was at the other side of the two lines. Nine Elms shed was very close by; this small area of Battersea was one of the few places where the coaling plant of one major engine shed could be seen from the top of another one. Stewarts Lane was the last of the three former Southern Railway depots to remain in use, surviving until the late 1990s; Nine Elms and Bricklayers Arms were completely obliterated many years earlier.

Originally known as Battersea or Longhedge, the shed was in the middle of a maze of lines just north of Factory Junction alongside the Longhedge Works and was the principal depot of the LC&DR. The sixteen-road, single-ended shed, built on the site in 1881 to replace the original semi-roundhouse, survived until the end of steam. It had an allocation of around a hundred engines, and became the main depot of the LC&DR's successor, the SE&CR.

When the Southern Railway embarked on the electrification of the South Eastern suburban lines during the 1920s, the importance of the depot declined, as did that of the ex-LB&SCR shed at Battersea Park. In 1932, it was decided to transfer the remaining engines to provide power for both Eastern and Central sections from one depot, and to close Battersea Park. Major improvements were needed to accommodate the combined allocation of around 170 engines from July 1934. With soft Government loans, the approach roads were modified, the turntable re-sited, new water columns installed and a 300-ton capacity mechanical coaling plant constructed. From completion of the work, the shed which was virtually a new depot, became known as Stewarts Lane.

The allocation was the highest of any shed on the Southern, its engines working all over the south-east of England. 'Lord Nelsons' and 'King Arthur' 4-6-0s powered the prestige 'Golden Arrow' and 'Night Ferry' boat trains as well as the other principal passenger services, to Margate, Ramsgate and Dover. Several dozen 'Moguls' and 0-6-0s, including twenty-four of the 'C Class, worked the large number of freight turns, while the ex-Brighton engines worked the services to Littlehampton, Bognor and Portsmouth. They also began to appear on the Eastern section trains; the Marsh 'H2' 'Atlantics' worked Victoria-Ramsgate trains and the 4-4-2Ts were frequently used on morning Victoria-Dover via Maidstone East trains.

The modern depot which began the war in 1939 suffered repeated heavy bombing, excessive traffic levels and virtually no maintenance. After the war ended, conditions not only failed to improve quickly but actually worsened and conditions steadily deteriorated until the end of steam working.

By 1949, the allocation had fallen to below 120, with the ex-LB&SCR classes taking the biggest hit, leaving only the 'E2' 0-6-0Ts. The 'Lord Nelsons' went too, concentrated on the Western Section, and prominent arrivals were fourteen 'Light Pacifics' and five 'Q1' 0-6-0s. There were thirteen each of the 'King Arthur' 4-6-0s, SE&CR 'H' Class 0-4-4Ts and 'C' Class 0-6-0s, twenty 'N' and 'U1' 2-6-0s, a dozen S&ECR design 4-4-0s and, surprisingly, eight ex-L&SWR 'T9' 4-4-0s, a type which had been allocated there since the late 1920s.

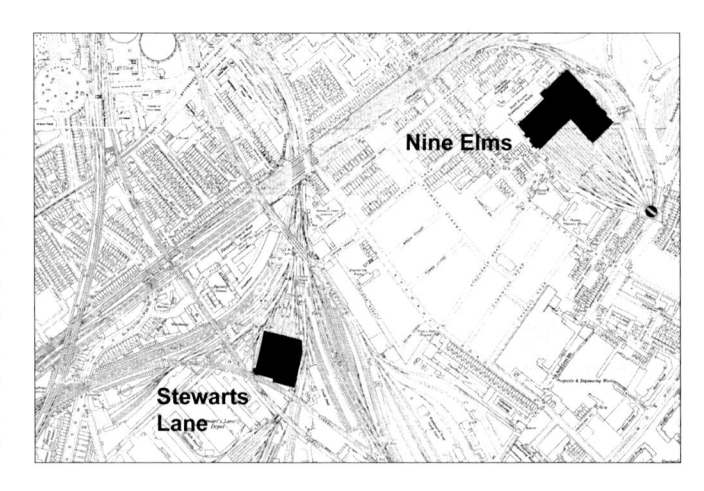

In the mid-1950s the patched-up depot continued to play an important part in the operation of the Southern Region, remaining responsible for the 'Golden Arrow' and the 'Night Ferry'. By November 1954, the allocation was down to 105, with notable newcomers in the shape of three 'Merchant Navy' Class and the two 'celebrity' Britannia 'Pacifics' used on the 'Night Ferry' and 'Golden Arrow', and several LM&SR design tank engines. The first Fairburn 2-6-4T had arrived for trials in April 1948, and ran extensive tests on the Victoria-Tunbridge Wells trains and similar commuter services. These proved a success and, from late 1950, new Brighton-built examples arrived to work trains to places such as Tunbridge Wells, Brighton and East Grinstead, filling in with empty stock work. The initial allocation, No's 42070-74 and 42080-84, only stayed for a few months but further examples were quickly transferred in and they worked alongside the very similar BR 'Standard' '4MT' 2-6-4Ts until 1959. The 2-6-4Ts were followed in 1951 by eight Ivatt Class '2' 2-6-2Ts, No's 41290-97, three of which stayed until the 1960s. In mid-1955, ten new Derby-built BR 'Standard' Class '5' 4-6-0s, No's 73080-89, arrived to replace a similar number of 'King Arthur' 4-6-0s which were transferred to the Western section.

Starting in 1957, the remains of Longhedge Works were swept away and a new three-road shed for electric locomotives constructed alongside the carriage and wagon repair shed. Third rail was installed in the yard in 1959 and other alterations were made to deal with the new motive power. The three Southern Railway-design electrics, No's 20001-3, were transferred from Brighton in March and the twenty-four new 'E5000's were delivered over the next eighteen months, followed by the first electro-diesels in 1962.

A total of 106 engines displaced by electrification were transferred in June 1959 from the South Eastern section, many from Stewarts Lane, to Nine Elms, including all of the 'E1', 'L' and 'L1' 4-4-0s and 'R1' 0-6-0Ts, plus twenty-five 'C' 0-6-0s, nine 'D1' 4-4-0s, seven 'H' 0-4-4Ts, two 'O1' 0-6-0s, nine 'Schools', and three 'Merchant Navy's. All of the section's 'King Arthur's and nine 'Standard' Class '5' 4-6-0s were moved from Stewarts Lane.

Most main line trains were now worked by electric multiple units, whilst BR&CW Type '3's based at Hither Green took over most of the shed's non-electric duties. There was still a reasonable steam presence until June 1961; six 'Light Pacifics' remained, together with five 'Schools' to handle the boat trains via Tonbridge and Maidstone East until electric services started on 12th June 1961. By the end of

1961, less than twenty steam locomotives remained: two 'Schools' 4-4-0s, one each of 'E1' 4-4-0, 'C' 0-6-0 and 'H' 0-4-4T and a few 'N' 2-6-0s, together with a couple of 'Light Pacifics', three 'Standard' 2-6-4Ts and two 'Standard' Class '4' 4-6-0s which were used on Central Section duties and for the summer Saturday inter-regional workings. There was also a 'Pannier' tank which had been transferred from Dover in November 1961.

Two of the sixteen covered roads were reduced from two roads per bay to one for diesel locomotive servicing in about 1959. At the end of the summer service, from September 1963, the last few steam engines were transferred away. The shed building remained largely intact until destroyed by fire in 1967, after which it was partly demolished, although the roof bays over the diesel servicing were retained.

To a casual visitor in post-steam days the area of the roofless steam shed became a dumping ground for PW equipment and although the entire fleet of forty-eight electro-diesel Class '73's were officially based there, they could be found scattered over the entire Region. As a spotter visiting the shed in this period, it was both fascinating, because of its past, and frustrating. Unlike many sheds in the 1970s, security at Stewarts Lane was well maintained and casual visits were not allowed; with full-time security guards manning the gatehouse, no amount of pleading would gain access. Therefore, visits were only possible with an official permit but at least these were issued free of charge. The main purpose for visits was usually to see the electro-diesels and, unlike most diesel classes, a very high proportion were out working PW trains at weekends. Usually there was a maximum of seven on shed at a weekend, often just two. One rumour was that a visit on a Saturday afternoon would reap rewards, as many of the fleet would return for diesel fuel before their Sunday jaunts. The shed and yard pilot was just one shunter and this worked at Victoria on parcels traffic at night.

Under British Railways, Stewarts Lane was coded 73A as the head of the District, but with the run-down it became 75D in June 1962.

'Pacifics'

Left: 'Battle of Britain' No. 21C154 *Lord Beaverbrook* entered traffic in January 1947 and retained its Bulleid number until February 1949, when it became No. 34054, keeping its malachite livery until 1951. Allocated to Stewarts Lane from new, the engine remained there until January 1949, when it was transferred to Salisbury. *The Lens of Sutton Association*

Below: No. 34071 *601 Squadron* coaled up at Stewarts Lane ready to work the 'Golden Arrow' on 18th October 1952. The 'Light Pacifics' worked the train from around 1948, until the two 'Britannias' took over at the end of 1951, although when one of these was not available a Bulleid engine substituted. New to Dover in April 1948, No. 34071 moved to Stewarts Lane in December 1949, before returning to Dover in June 1955. The engine, the first of the class with a wide, wedge-fronted cab, was rebuilt in 1960.

4-4-0s

All of the 'Schools' were given the so-called 'lesser' passenger livery of lined black between October 1948 and July 1952. No. 30912 *Downside* received one of the later variants in May 1950, with low cab and tender lining, 10 inch numbers, lined splashers and the smaller version of the first BR emblem positioned centrally between the horizontal lining. It was allocated to Ramsgate at the date of this picture on 4th April 1954 and was transferred no less than twenty-one times during its thirty years in service.

No. 31504 was built in 1906 at Ashford as an SE&CR 'E' Class 4-4-0 and was one of ten engines rebuilt to an 'E1' by Beyer, Peacock in 1920, following the successful modification of one of the class in 1919. The footplate over the driving wheels was raised and the Wainwright cab was replaced with a standard Maunsell type. A new larger firebox was fitted and the slide valves were replaced with piston valves. It was allocated to Stewarts Lane throughout the British Railways period, up to its withdrawal in February 1958.

CHAPTER 7 - STEWARTS LANE

Wainwright's Class 'E' 4-4-0s followed on from his successful 'D' Class, with twenty-six built between 1905 and 1909. In 1919, Maunsell decided to rebuild one, No. 179, and considerably changed the appearance of the engine. The footplate over the driving wheels was raised and the cab was replaced with a standard Maunsell type. A new larger firebox was fitted and the slide valves were replaced with piston valves. This, the first 'E1', was rebuilt at Ashford and proved successful and therefore ten more, including No. 31019, were rebuilt in 1920 by Beyer, Peacock & Co. No. 31019 was at its home shed on 18th October 1952 and stayed at Stewarts Lane until the mass clear out of steam in June 1959, when it was transferred to Nine Elms.

No. 31776, photographed at Stewarts Lane on 29th May 1957, was one of the 'L' Class 4-4-0s built in Germany by A. Borsig in June 1914. When R.E.L Maunsell was appointed as Chief Mechanical Engineer of the SE&CR in 1913, he modified the new express design which his predecessor, H.S. Wainwright, had been developing. The most noticeable changes were a new chimney and a larger cab roof, extending to the rear of the footplate and supported on round pillars. The first twelve engines were built by Beyer, Peacock and Co. of Manchester. However, because more engines were needed for the 1914 summer service, ten were built by A Borsig of Berlin since Beyer, Peacock were unable to complete the order within this timescale. All of the engines had Belpaire fireboxes but the British-built ones had Robinson superheaters, whereas the German-built ones had the Schmidt type. These were the only German express steam locomotives built for a British railway and were shipped to Dover in knock-down form; the frames and boilers were then erected at Ashford by Borsig's own workers. No. 31776 was allocated to Brighton until June 1959, when it was transferred to Nine Elms; it was withdrawn in February 1961.

CHAPTER 7 - STEWARTS LANE

Tank engines

A very clean No. 41291 poses at Stewarts Lane on 18th October 1952. The LM&SR designed Ivatt Class '2' 2-6-2Ts arrived on the Southern Region in 1951-52, with No's 41290-41297 and 41313-15 going to Stewarts Lane, and No's 41298-41303 to Bricklayers Arms. No. 41291 was the second of the class built with enlarged cylinder bores, increasing the tractive effort from 17,400lbs to 18,510lbs, and a taller and thinner chimney than on the earlier engines. The guard irons were also modified, in a much neater and less conspicuous position mounted on the pony truck rather than extending downward from the frames. A more subtle change was made to the profile of the cab roof where it met the cab side, resulting in an almost horizontal instead of a sloping rain strip. No. 41291 was at Stewarts Lane from new in September 1951 until March 1963, when it was transferred to Exmouth Junction. Its stay in Devon was quite short and it went to the Somerset & Dorset at Templecombe in June 1965.

One of the original five LB&SCR Billinton 'E2' 0-6-0Ts built in 1914, No. 32104 at its home shed on 14th March 1953; it was transferred to Bricklayers Arms in June 1957. In 1950, Stewarts Lane had eight of the ten engines in the class on its books, an inheritance from the former LB&SCR shed at Battersea which had closed in the 1930s. When the first *Thomas the Tank Engine* book was published, the artist who illustrated it based *Thomas* on the 'E2' and the Reverend W. Audrey apparently described the engine as the eleventh member of the class. However, unlike No. 32104, he had front tank extensions, a modification to the original design made on the last five engines. In the background is the distinctive Hampton's Depository. A familiar landmark for commuters into Victoria since 1903, this massive red brick and terracotta building, curved to follow the railway, was built as a furniture store and workshops for Hampton & Sons, the Pall Mall East cabinet-makers and furniture dealers. It was struck by German flying bombs in 1944, though the demolished section, on the far right, was rebuilt. Hamptons was closed in 1956 and the site was taken over by the Decca music and electronics company, and its Special Products Division was based there between 1964 and 1978; the building is still in use today, as a self-storage facility.

'W' Class 2-6-4T No. 31921 at Stewarts Lane on 28th April 1962 alongside BR 'Standard' 2-6-4T No. 80148. No. 31921 was at Norwood Junction from November 1957 and used on the cross-London transfer freights until withdrawn in June 1963. Stewarts Lane had three 'W's on its books in early British Railways days. The heavy footsteps to the rear of the outside cylinders to provide access to the tank fillers was a noticeable feature of the class. No. 80148 was allocated to Brighton from new in November 1956 until June 1963, when it was transferred to Feltham.

'P' Class 0-6-0T No. 31558 is dwarfed by the 300-ton Stewarts Lane coaling plant. Eight of these diminutive engines were built by the SE&CR at Ashford Works in 1909-10 for light branch and push-pull duties, replacing steam railmotors that had proved under-powered for the work. They did not prove any better than the railmotors and by 1913 all were working as shed pilots or on light shunting duties. No. 31558 was built in June 1910 and was the last Southern Railway locomotive to be renumbered, in July 1953. It was withdrawn in February 1960, and scrapped although half of the class survived into preservation. No. 31558 spent its last five years at Stewarts Lane, having moved there from Brighton in May 1955.

No. 42087 in the yard at Stewarts Lane on 14th August 1958. The bridge in the distance carried the LC&DR main line into Victoria. The first LM&SR Fairburn 2-6-4Ts to work on the Southern Region were during the 1948, trials when No's 42198 and 42199 were transferred. The former worked from Nine Elms and the latter from Stewarts Lane, on a series of trials between April and June covering the main suburban duties worked by each shed. The two engines then went to March shed on the Eastern Region and two ex-L&NER 'L1' 2-6-4Ts took their place but these proved less suitable than the LM&SR engines. New members of the class, built at Brighton in late 1950 and early 1951, went in groups to several Central and Eastern section sheds, with Stewarts Lane receiving No's 42070-74 and 42080-4 but all except the last two had moved away by the middle of 1951, being replaced by No's 42089-91 in early 1952 and No. 42088 at the end of 1954. It was not until November 1956 that No's 42086 and 42087 arrived at Stewarts Lane. No. 42087, built at Brighton in March 1951, was allocated there from late 1956 until July 1959, when it returned to its previous shed at Tunbridge Wells West. It left the Southern Region in November 1959, moving to Neasden.

A condensing-fitted Fowler Class '3' 2-6-2T was an unusual visitor to Stewarts Lane as late as 14th May 1961. No. 40024 from Kentish Town was in its final year in service, being withdrawn in March 1962.

Diesels and electrics

The second of the Bulleid-designed Southern Railway electric locomotives, No. 20002 at Stewarts Lane on 28th April 1962. It is in original condition without air horns and route indicator panel and has a pantograph for yard working, although these were rarely used and were taken off in in the mid-1960s. All three of the locomotives were transferred to Stewarts Lane from Brighton in March 1959 and stayed until August 1966, when they returned to the south coast shed. By the late 1930s, the Southern Railway began to consider electrical power for freight and express passenger work in addition to its widespread use of multiple units. Two experimental Co-Co mixed traffic electric locomotives were designed jointly by Oliver Bulleid, the Chief Mechanical Engineer, who was responsible for external design and the mechanical parts, and Alfred Raworth, the Chief Electrical Engineer, who was responsible for the electrical systems. They had to overcome a major problem with third-rail pick-up locomotives, commonly referred to as 'gapping', which gave rise to the 'Booster' nickname for the locomotives. This arose because the distance between the outer pickups was much shorter than on the multiple unit sets and therefore the traction supply could be lost when the gap between conductor rails was longer than the distance between the locomotive's pickups. The solution adopted was instead of the electrical supply powering the traction motors directly, it drove two motor generator sets fitted with heavy flywheels. This enabled power to the traction motors to be maintained by the generator sets (boosters), which were driven by the flywheel when the traction supply was interrupted. The locomotives were solidly constructed with cabs at each end similar to contemporary EMUs such as the early 'Sheba' '4-SUB'.

24 Bo-Bo electric locomotives of 2,552hp, designed to haul freight trains of up to 900 tons and heavy passenger trains including the 'Night Ferry', were built at Doncaster for the Kent Coast electrification and were originally numbered E5001 to E5024, becoming Class '71' under TOPS. As with the three Southern Railway electric locomotives, Nos 20001-3, booster equipment was fitted to overcome the problems with "gapping" on the third rail caused by the short distance between the collector shoes. To allow safe working in sidings, a single pantograph was mounted centrally on the roof. No. E5021 at Stewarts Lane in 1961 was in its original livery with a horizontal red stripe along the body side and no yellow warning panel, as delivered from Doncaster in July 1960. It was taken out of service for conversion at Crewe Works to an electro-diesel in May 1967, the last of the ten to be modified. When completed in June 1968 it emerged as No. E6110 and became No. 74010 in 1974. The conversions were not successful and No. 74010 was withdrawn along with the other seven then remaining Class '74's at the end of 1977.

CHAPTER 7 - STEWARTS LANE

As early as 1947, the Southern Railway was considering a locomotive capable of being powered by two different sources – traction current picked up from the third rail and also from an on-board diesel generator set, albeit at reduced power. This would allow the locomotive to operate in non-electrified sidings and docks, and also when the traction current was switched off during engineering and track possessions. The dual power concept evolved throughout the 1950s, and in 1959 six 1,600 hp locomotives were authorised incorporating the 600 hp English Electric 4SRKT engine which powered the Hastings line diesel-electric multiple units. They were built at Eastleigh in 1962 and numbered E6001-6, becoming No's 73001-6 under TOPS. They were designed to work in multiple with all the types of electro-pneumatically braked Southern Region multiple units and had air, vacuum and electro-pneumatic brake systems. A very useful feature was that the locomotives could change power supply at speed, since the diesel could be started and stopped, and the pick-ups raised and lowered on the move. The design was immediately successful and a further thirty were ordered in June 1963 and, soon after, another thirteen were authorised. Seen here wearing the original green livery with a grey stripe and coaching stock style BR roundel, the second electro-diesel No. E6002 was photographed at Stewarts Lane in 1962, having entered traffic in March. of that year It became No. 73002 in 1974 and was withdrawn in 1993, after spending the previous three years in and out of store. It is now on static display at the Dean Forest Railway in Gloucestershire.

No. E5018 was completed in June 1960 at Eastleigh, having been sent incomplete from Doncaster because of a shortage of materials. It was renumbered to No. E5003 in December 1968 after the original locomotive carrying that number was converted to an electro-diesel. It became No. 71003 under TOPS and after storage for over a year was withdrawn in November 1977. Next to it, No. E6001, the first electro-diesel, had been delivered from Eastleigh in February 1962. It was used by Merseyrail as a rescue locomotive/shunter from November 1995, renumbered as No. 73901, and was bought for preservation in 2002 and, like its erstwhile classmate No. E6002, is currently at the Dean Forest Railway.

The original No. E5000, completed in December 1958, and renumbered to No. E5024 in December 1962, at Stewarts Lane on 27th July 1963 with No. E5012 in front of the three-road electric locomotive servicing depot built for the Kent Coast Electrification in 1959. Note the contrasting grills on opposing sides of these electrics and the different positioning of the stock numbers. Both have lost their red body side stripe but still do not have yellow warning panels. No. E5024 was converted to an electro-diesel between October 1966 and February 1968, becoming No. E6104, but No. E5012 remained a straight electric until withdrawn as No. 71012 in 1977.

CHAPTER 7 - STEWARTS LANE

The former steam running shed on 19th June 1964; the two bays on the right were reduced from two roads per bay to one for diesel locomotive servicing in about 1959. The viaduct behind the shed carries the South London Line.

When the three-road electric locomotive shed was built for the Kent Coast Electrification in 1959, the existing carriage shed, which was formerly a Pullman car depot, was extended to cover fourteen roads to accommodate the electric multiple units, as shown in this photograph taken in the early 1970s from the staff footbridge spanning the throat of the carriage shed. Train movements could be so intense that provision of a footbridge was the only way to navigate efficiently and safely across the depot, especially at peak times. Motor Luggage Van No. 68003 peeps out of the shed, with a variety of EMU types inside behind it, including '4-CEP' units Nos 7108 and 7137 and '4-EPB' No. 5237.

8 – Waterloo

Until the rebuilding of Euston in the 1960s, Waterloo was the only London terminus built in the 20th Century.

The first terminus of what became the London & South Western Railway in 1839 was opened at Nine Elms in 1838 but this was too far out of the capital and Waterloo station was opened in 1848. From the beginning, commuter traffic was very important and so the L&SWR constructed a 1½ mile extension, mainly on a brick viaduct with over 200 arches to minimise disturbance to existing properties, from Nine Elms Junction to a terminus on the South Bank by Hungerford Bridge. In the event, the L&SWR only ever reached the City via the Waterloo & City underground line, nicknamed 'The Drain', which opened in 1898.

In 1864, a 5-chain connection to the LC&DR London Bridge-Charing Cross line was provided, as an extension of an empty carriage line; this was taken out of use in 1911. In the final decades of the 19th Century, the station was extended in piecemeal fashion, increasing to eighteen platforms in 1885.

A further 6½ acres of land were purchased at the turn of the new century and a completely new station was designed, inspired by contemporary American railroad termini. As built, it had twenty-one platforms, with a wide passenger concourse and a long frontage containing railway offices. This major redevelopment began in 1902, with the first five new platforms completed in 1909 but then took many more years to complete and was not formally opened until March 1922. The station occupied a site of 24½ acres, the largest in Britain.

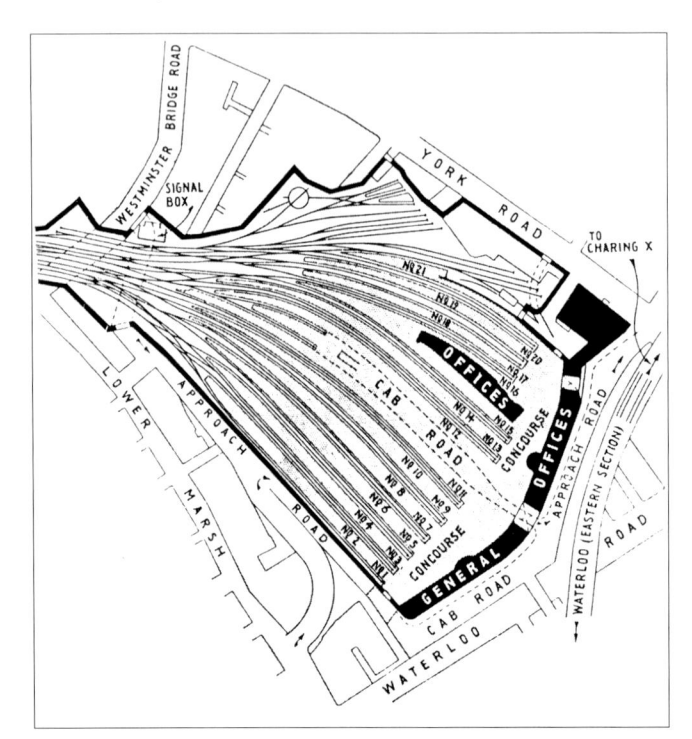

The station layout after the completion of the rebuilding in 1922.

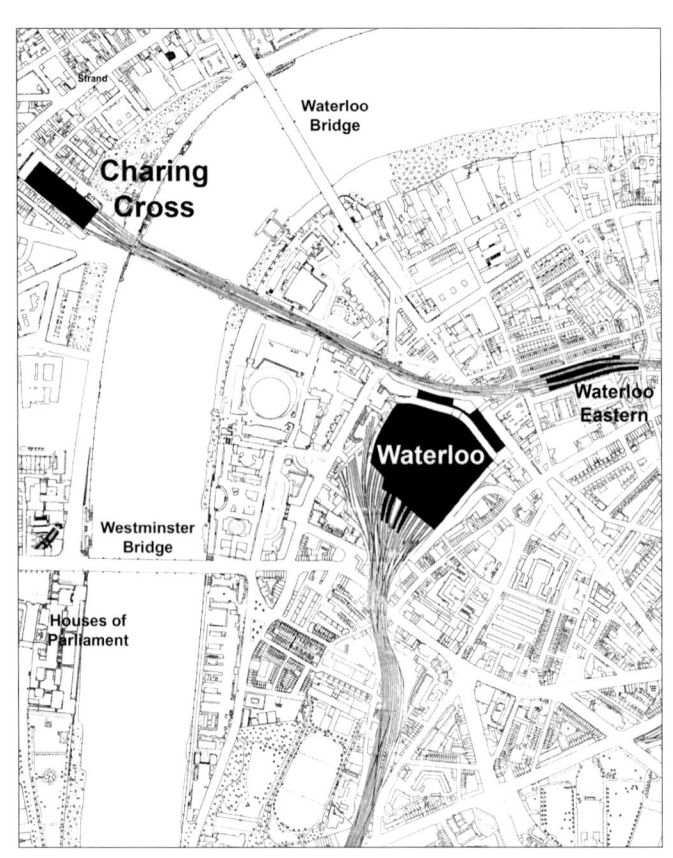

The first third rail electric services began in 1915 and all eight running lines were soon equipped for electric working, although only twelve platforms could be used by the trains. Over the next two decades, further suburban lines were electrified and this resulted in a rearrangement of the approach roads in 1936, including a new flyover at Wimbledon to eliminate crossing movements at the station throat. The first main line electric services began in 1937, to Portsmouth, but it was not until 1967 that the route to Bournemouth was finally electrified.

In 1961, the station was the subject of the critically acclaimed film *Terminus*, produced by John Schlesinger for British Transport Films. It was an early example of the 'fly-on-the-wall' documentary, following the comings and goings of passengers and staff during an ordinary working day, although professional actors were used in various staged shots.

The next major development was the 400 metre long, five platform Waterloo International Terminal, built for Eurostar services at a cost of around £135 million on the site of the old Windsor line platforms No's 16 to 21 and the sidings alongside. An expensive connection at Stewarts Lane also had to be built to link it to the route to the Channel Tunnel. The terminal was opened in 1994 but closed in November 2007 when the new international station at St. Pancras was opened. The platforms will soon be returned to domestic use as part of the main station, providing an increase in capacity of around thirty per cent.

CHAPTER 8 - WATERLOO

A bird's eye view of Waterloo in 1966, wearing what must have been the largest ever version of the British Railways roundel. The York Road entrance, known as the Victory Arch, had been dedicated as a memorial to railwaymen who lost their lives in the First World War. The former SE&CR line from London Bridge into Charing Cross passed within a few feet of the main entrance; Waterloo Eastern station is out of the picture on the left.

An interesting view showing the sidings at the side of the Windsor platforms. The hydraulically powered Armstrong lift in the centre enabled Waterloo & City underground coaches to be removed from 'The Drain' for servicing. For many years coal wagons were also taken down the lift carrying coal for the independent power station for the line and the station boiler house. Immediately behind the lift is a Cinema Coach amongst the motley collection of wagons and vans in the sidings, along with several EMUs. Most of the area in the foreground was used for the approach roads to the International Station which opened in 1994 – the station itself did not extend much, if anything, beyond the existing boundary of the old Windsor Line platforms.

Passengers stream from '4-SUB' No. 4369 after its arrival at Platform 2 in a scene which could have been taken from the classic 1961 award-winning John Schlesinger *Terminus* documentary film. Note that the platform numbers are still in Southern Railway style.

1950s steam

Class 'T9' No. 30119 at Waterloo on 26th March 1950, on what according to the headcode discs was an ECS duty to Clapham Junction. The locomotive was built at Nine Elms in 1899 and allocated there until June 1951; it was withdrawn at the end of 1952. The malachite green paint finish and SR 'sunshine' style BR number and lettering were applied during an 'A' overhaul at Eastleigh completed in June 1948. Note the engine number painted on the rear of the 4,000 gallon, eight-wheeled 'Watercart' tender.

Waterloo handled many boat trains to and from Southampton, as illustrated by No. 30778 *Sir Pelleas* setting off with a United States Lines 'Statesman' special on 17th June 1954. The North British Locomotive Company-built 'King Arthur' was allocated to Nine Elms from July 1953 until withdrawn in May 1959. Alongside is another 'King Arthur', Eastleigh-built No. 30747 *Elaine* which was at Eastleigh from May 1951 until it was taken out of traffic in October 1956. The name *Elaine* passed to a BR Standard Class '5' 4-6-0, No. 73119, in 1959.

The 'Brittany Express' was a seasonal train, travelling Up from Southampton Quay in the morning and Down from Waterloo in the evening; it ran for ten years from 1954 until 1964. A young spotter admires 'King Arthur' No. 30784 *Sir Nerovens* as it waits for departure in the mid-1950s. Like *Sir Pelleas* above, it was another of the 'Scotch Arthurs', built by the North British Locomotive Company at Glasgow in August 1925. The engine had carried a rather strange-looking large diameter chimney until late 1954 and was allocated to Eastleigh from February 1951, until withdrawn in October 1959. The original Western section 'Arthurs' all had 5,000 gallon, double-bogie, flared-top tenders.

This very clean Nine Elms 'Light Pacific', devoid of route indicator discs but still carrying the tail lamp from its train. Light Engines carried the headcode for their outgoing train on the tender, and this was then transferred to the front of the engine by the firemen, which he hasn't yet done here. The first coach also still has its tail lamp from the ECS working from Clapham Junction. This would not have been removed until the train locomotive had arrived, so the fireman was probably still coupling-up at this point – on the ex-L&SWR lines this was the fireman's job rather than the shunter's. The picture was probably taken shortly after No. 34063 *229 Squadron* had completed a Heavy Classified repair in May 1954. It had originally been allocated to Ramsgate and then Stewarts Lane, before moving to Nine Elms in March 1950.

CHAPTER 8 - WATERLOO

With the curved roof of the Royal Festival Hall in the left background, 'Merchant Navy' No. 35021 *New Zealand Line* is about to depart at the head of 'The Royal Wessex' in 1955. The name was introduced in 1951 in honour of the Festival of Britain and the train left Waterloo at 4.35pm, calling at Winchester, Southampton and Brockenhurst before finally reaching Bournemouth at 6.55pm. No. 35021 was built in 1948 with a wedge-shaped cab, three side windows and a fabricated rear truck. The frames and cylinders were built at Ashford, the boiler and tender at Brighton, and construction of the remaining parts and final assembly was done at Eastleigh. It had been repainted from BR blue into green in February 1952 and the tender side sheets were cut back to make it easier to fill from a water column and to reduce corrosion due to trapped water. *New Zealand Line* was rebuilt in 1959, whilst the tender, No. 3342, is still in existence today, running behind preserved No. 35028 *Clan Line*.

Prototype Diesels

The Southern Railway designed a main line diesel-electric prior to Nationalisation but lost the 'race' to get the first one into service to the LM&SR by three years. The second of these locomotives, No. 10202, is seen here ready to depart from Waterloo on 15th December 1951. It was built at Ashford and put into traffic exactly three months earlier, on 15th September. The Southern locomotives used the same English Electric 16SVT engine as the LM&SR machines, although developing 1,750hp rather than 1,600hp. They were longer and heavier, and had to be carried on four-axle bogies, with the outer axle an idler in a 1-Co-Co-1 wheel arrangement, compared to the six-wheeled, all-powered type used on No's 10000/1. This eight-wheeled bogie was later adopted for the BR English Electric and Sulzer Type '4' designs. No. 10202 was transferred to the London Midland Region in April 1955 and was withdrawn at the end of 1963, after being stored unserviceable from November 1962.

Although No. 10000 was outshopped before Nationalisation, its 'twin' No. 10001 did not appear until July 1948 and therefore did not have the cast 'LMS' insignia that was given to the earlier locomotive, although the numbers were cast. The two diesel-electrics moved to the Southern Region at Nine Elms in early 1953 and were employed on expresses from Waterloo to Bournemouth, Weymouth and Exeter. Carrying a Waterloo-Bournemouth headcode, No. 10001 was photographed backing out of the station in July 1954. The headcode for its next working had been put up and it was probably going over either to North Sidings for refuelling or to the two loading docks between the country end of Platforms 11 and 12 to await its next working.

CHAPTER 8 - WATERLOO

No. 10001 departing from Waterloo on 27th May 1954. Along with No. 10000, it had moved to the Southern Region in early 1953 when it was decided to concentrate all the prototype main line diesels there. The LM&SR 'twins' remained on the Southern Region after the third SR design locomotive, No. 10203, entered service in April 1954, although they were taken off the prestige trains because of poor reliability. No. 10001 had been at Brighton Works for repairs between June 1953 and February 1954, and emerged with an electric speedometer, which can be seen on the middle axle of the rear bogie; it also received the 6P/5F power classification and a small version of the BR emblem instead of its original large emblem but kept its black livery. The two locomotives were transferred back to the London Midland Region in April 1955.

The third main line diesel locomotive authorised by the Southern Railway was not completed until March 1954, almost three years after No. 10202. The delay allowed a more powerful 2,000hp version of the 16SVT engine to be used and other improvements from the first two locomotives were incorporated, including an increase in the maximum permitted speed from 85mph to 90mph (the first two, No's 10201 and 10202, were originally geared for 110mph but were later re-geared). After completion of testing, No. 10203 commenced revenue earning service on 10th May, before going on display at the International Railway Conference Exhibition at Willesden between 25th May and 4th June, hence its 'showroom' condition in this picture taken on 17th June, as the hatted railway officials engage in discussion before departure. No. 10203 was transferred to the London Midland Region in August 1955 and was withdrawn at the end of 1963, after being stored unserviceable from October 1962. It was in many ways the fore-runner of the 200 English Electric Type '4's which had the same 2,000hp engine and eight-wheeled bogies.

1960s steam

'West Country' No. 34036 *Westward Ho* arriving with the 'Bournemouth Belle' on 6th July 1967. Rebuilt in August 1960, it had been transferred to Nine Elms from Eastleigh in June 1966 for its final year in service; No. 34036 was withdrawn within a few days of this photograph when Southern steam came to an end. Note the Second World War bomb damage in the foreground, still unrepaired over twenty years after the war had ended.

The approach to Waterloo from Nine Elms Junction was on a viaduct with over 200 brick arches. 'Schools' No. 30902 *Wellington* is departing from Waterloo on the Down Main Through line in 1962. It was allocated to Nine Elms from November 1960 until withdrawal at the end of 1962. *Wellington* was repainted from lined black to green in April 1959 and was fitted with AWS during the same General Overhaul.

An interesting collection of discs and reporting numbers on the smokebox door of BR 'Standard' Class '4' 2-6-0 No. 76013. The 255 pasted on a rectangular board hung from the top lamp bracket was the train number. The headcode indicates a Weymouth to Waterloo via Ringwood service. No. 76013 went new to Eastleigh in April 1953, where it stayed until September 1964, moving then to Bournemouth. The Eastleigh Class '4's regularly worked to Waterloo on the Saturday Lymington Pier boat trains. The engine is paired with a small Type 'BR2' 3,500 gallon tender with inset bunker.

Another of the Eastleigh Class '4' 2-6-0s, No. 76064, which unlike No. 76013 above, has a large Type 'BR1B' 4,725 gallon tender. It was always allocated to Eastleigh, from new in July 1956 until withdrawn in July 1967. It is arriving at Platform 7, which was normally the lowest numbered platform used by steam-powered trains, as there were no water columns available on Platforms 1 to 5 at the buffer stops.

CHAPTER 8 - WATERLOO

The complex pointwork needed to provide access to the twenty-one platforms at Waterloo shows up clearly in this view, as an unidentified 2-6-0 backs out of the station in 1962. In the background on the right are two '4-COR' multiple units at Platforms 12 and 13, whilst a "Pannier" tank on empty coaching stock duties stands at Platform 10.

No. 34016 *Bodmin* on a Bournemouth express in 1962, with six-car restaurant set No. 298 at the front of the train. The tail lamp on the front has not yet been replaced by a disc but this is probably the 11.30am to Bournemouth West, which was an Eastleigh turn at the time. Rebuilt in 1958, No. 34016 was one of no less than eighteen 'Light Pacifics' rescued from Barry Docks. *Bodmin* was restored at the Mid-Hants Railway and ran on the main line for a time but has not been in use for several years and is currently awaiting overhaul. It was allocated to Eastleigh from May 1961 until withdrawn in June 1964. The speedometer and AWS equipment were fitted in August 1960.

A 'Battle of Britain' is admired by the spotters as it arrives from either Basingstoke or possibly, Eastleigh. No. 34089 *602 Squadron* was one of the later rebuilds, in November 1960, and carries a 72B Salisbury shedplate, where it moved to in September 1963 from Brighton. It was the last steam engine to be officially repaired at Eastleigh, in October 1966.

CHAPTER 8 - WATERLOO

The signal box controlling Waterloo was brought into use in October 1936 and had a 309-lever, electrically interlocked frame in three sections, for 'Main Local', 'Main Through' and 'Windsor Lines'. It was replaced by a new installation at Wimbledon in 1990 and was demolished in 1991. In front, 'M7' Class 0-4-4T No. 30321 is shunting an L&NER parcels van. Built in 1900 at Nine Elms, it was one of the short framed 'M7s' with the front sandboxes below the running plate. After spending many years in the West Country at Exmouth Junction and Barnstaple, No. 30321 came to Nine Elms in late 1952 and was withdrawn from there in September 1962.

The big Class 'H16' 4-6-2Ts spent most of their time on freight work but were regular visitors to Waterloo, mostly on weekend ECS duties. In this case, No. 30518 is working milk empties back to Clapham Junction, after they had been unloaded at the United Dairies depot alongside Vauxhall station.

The 'M7' 0-4-4Ts employed for many years on ECS movements to and from Clapham Junction had to work especially hard, since they had an allowance of only ten minutes for the journey out to the carriage sidings. No. 30039 is certainly producing a spectacular show of smoke across the platform ends as it gets underway here. Built in 1898 at Nine Elms, it was one of the short framed 'M7s' with the front sandboxes on the splashers and was allocated to Nine Elms for its final years, from March 1960 until withdrawal in March 1963. The building under construction and nearing completion is the Shell Centre, which was built on the site used for the 1951 Festival of Britain. It consisted of a twenty-seven-storey tower, three nine-storey buildings nearer to the station and another separate block on the other side of the Waterloo Eastern to Charing Cross line. At the time, the tower was the tallest storied building in Britain and the centre was the largest office block, by floor area, in Europe.

CHAPTER 8 - WATERLOO

An unidentified 'Lord Nelson' 4-6-0 backs down on to its train at Platform 9 in 1962. This was probably the 10.54 Salisbury stopping service, because the tender is carrying the Waterloo-Plymouth headcode and this was an Eastleigh 'Nelson' turn at the time. The occupants in the flats had an excellent view of proceedings at Waterloo, although they must have been glad when steam operation ended in July 1967. The large arrow on the left pointing to Waterloo acted as a running-in board for the benefit of passengers, because the platforms did not have nameboards.

'Schools' No. 30934 *St. Lawrence*, approaching Platform 7 at Waterloo as a Bulleid 'Pacific' waits for departure on the 'Bournemouth Belle' in 1962, was fitted with a Lemaître multiple jet exhaust in 1940. It was transferred from Ashford to Basingstoke in October 1961 and was withdrawn in December 1962. As with several of the class, No. 30934 ran in lined black throughout most of the 1950s and was only repainted green in February 1960.

Although the headcode shown is for a Waterloo-Plymouth service, this is almost certainly a stopping train to Salisbury leaving Platform 7 headed by Urie 'S15' 4-6-0 No. 30512. The locomotive was built by the L&SWR at Eastleigh in 1921, primarily for working freight, and was a smaller-wheeled version of the 'H15' 4-6-0. Fitted with AWS in June 1962, after withdrawal in April 1964, No. 30512 was sold to Woodham Brothers at Barry but was destined to be one of the few unfortunate engines that were actually cut-up at the scrapyard.

'Merchant Navy' No. 35007 *Aberdeen Commonwealth* passes classmate No. 35012 *United States Line*, whilst being sandwiched by departing and arriving EMUs on either side as it gets underway with a West of England express. The same headcode was carried on all trains to the area as far as Exeter Central, even if there was no Plymouth portion. No. 35007 was rebuilt in 1958 and when withdrawn in July 1967, was sold for scrap.

The appearance of an 'H16' 4-6-2T such as No. 30517 on a summer Saturday diagram provided a welcome change from the regular 'M7' 0-4-4Ts on ECS working. In 1921, the L&SWR built four 4-8-0T 'hump' shunters, the 'G16' Class, to work its new marshalling yard at Feltham. At the same time, five engines in a 4-6-2T version, the 'H16' Class, which were primarily intended for goods traffic between Feltham and Brent (Midland Railway), and Willesden (L&NWR), was introduced. They shared many components including the bogies, boiler and motion. Both classes had a coal capacity of 3½ tons and a low water capacity of only 2,000 gallons, reflecting their limited sphere of operation. The main differences between them were the driving wheels, which were six inches larger on the 'H16' than those on the 'G16' at 5ft 7ins, 21ins x 28ins cylinders instead of 22ins x 28ins, and a radial truck. All five 'H16's were withdrawn in November 1962.

Immaculate 'Merchant Navy' No. 35028 Clan Line ready for departure with the 'Bournemouth Belle' on 8th August 1964. The all-Pullman train commenced running in 1931 and after the war was one of the first titled trains in the country to be restored to the time table, in October 1947. It was one of the heaviest trains on the route, loading up to twelve Pullman cars weighing 500 tons and usually hauled by a 'Merchant Navy' 'Pacific'. Until February 1960, the stock was stabled at Stewarts Lane along with that for the 'Golden Arrow' and after that, both sets of coaches were kept at Clapham Junction.

CHAPTER 8 - WATERLOO 123

Five LM&SR-designed Ivatt Class '2' 2-6-2Ts released by other Southern Region sheds went to Nine Elms for ECS work in the last year of Southern steam. One of them was No. 41319, which was the last Crewe-built Class '2' tank. From new in June 1952, it had been allocated to several Central and Eastern section sheds before arriving at Nine Elms in March 1967; it was withdrawn on 9th July 1967, the final day of SR steam. The chimneys on the last thirty engines were of larger diameter than the 41290-99 series and were almost a stretched version of the original shorter chimney on No's 41200-89. Two of the three towers at the Houses of Parliament are visible in the background, Victoria Tower on the left and the shorter Central Tower to the right.

The tank engine which had brought in the stock from Clapham Junction would bank the departing train out of the station, before dropping back onto one of the loading dock roads to wait for its next ECS working out to Clapham. On 21st March 1963, BR Standard Class '3' 2-6-2T No. 82019 has already shut off steam after the outgoing express has left it behind. No. 82019 had been at Exmouth Junction from new in 1952 and arrived at Nine Elms in November 1962 after two months at Eastleigh; it was withdrawn in July 1967.

By the final years of Southern steam, little attention was given to the condition of the engines used on ECS work, as shown here by No. 82028 on 3rd March 1966. This was originally a North Eastern Region engine, moving to Guildford in late 1963, then to Bournemouth in January 1964, before arriving at Nine Elms later that year in September. It was withdrawn in September 1966.

From the first week of the 1965 summer time table, there was a marked increase in the use of 'foreign' locomotives on South Western domestic services following their arrival on inter-regional trains. Examples included Stanier Class '5' 4-6-0 No. 45046 from Crewe South, which worked the 21.24pm Bournemouth to Eastleigh local on 16th June 1965 and the 15.35pm Waterloo-Bournemouth the next day. It was then used on a number of occasions until the end of the month on a diagram covering the 08.01am Eastleigh-Waterloo and 15.35pm Waterloo-Bournemouth. The offset and lowered top lamp bracket, moved for safety reasons when working 'under the wires' on the London Midland Region, allowed a more or less accurate Waterloo-Bournemouth headcode to be displayed.

CHAPTER 8 - WATERLOO

In the days when domestic freight and parcels traffic was still moved mainly by the railway, Platform 13 is full of trolleys and also the new BRUTEs (British Rail Universal Trolley Equipment), which were first used by the Western Region in 1964. They were designed to save time and reduce handling of small parcels by loading them into a wheeled platform with mesh sides, which could be wheeled on or off the train using a metal ramp. 'West Country' No. 34004 *Yeovil* arrives with an express from Bournemouth in 1966. It was transferred from Stewarts Lane to the Western section at Eastleigh in May 1961, and in October 1965 to Bournemouth. The pre-Nationalisation parcels stock in the picture is typical of the period: Southern Railway four-wheeled 'PMV' and 'CCT's, an LM&SR six-wheeled 'Stove R' providing guards accommodation, and a GWR four-wheeled 'Fruit D'. Note that the third rail stopped well short of the stop blocks to allow enginemen to oil round and check locomotives at track level without the danger of electrocution. This was not a problem for EMUs which had a bus line feeding motors off the third rail but the third rail had to be extended to the stop blocks after the Bournemouth electrification to prevent the electric locomotives becoming 'gapped'. This was done on all main line Platforms 6 to 15 but Platforms 1 to 5 were not altered and remain this way today.

One of the handful of 'Light Pacifics' built at Eastleigh rather than Brighton, 'West Country' No. 34102 *Lapford* only entered traffic in February 1950. It was working the LCGB 'The Bridport Belle Rail Tour', with 'Battle of Britain' No. 34057 *Biggin Hill* on 22nd January 1967. Neither of the two unrebuilt 'Pacifics' survived into preservation. The pair worked through to Salisbury, where No. 34102 came off and No. 34057 carried on alone to Westbury. However, they were reunited for the return from Salisbury to Waterloo. The tour was beset by numerous problems, not least the discovery of a dead body in one of the toilets. Apparently, this had occurred when the stock was used on an Up service the previous day but after a short, seven minute stop at Basingstoke to remove the body, the tour continued. The contrast to what would happen in similar circumstances today is enormous.

Modern traction

A change in regional boundaries brought the Waterloo-Exeter line west of Salisbury under Western Region control from January 1963. The following year, it was announced that the Class 'D1000' 'Western' diesel-hydraulics were to be moved onto the Paddington-Bristol and Paddington-Plymouth services, displacing 'Warships' and releasing the older class for other duties, including dieselisation of the Southern Region Exeter-Salisbury-Waterloo service. A regular interval pattern of semi-fasts between Waterloo and Exeter was introduced from 7th September 1964, to replace the express service hauled for many years by the Bulleid 'Pacifics'. No. D829 *Magpie* arrived at Salisbury for crew training at the beginning of June and was replaced after a week by No. D819. Three return trips each day were made to Basingstoke using a train of thirteen condemned coaches. The roster included a twice-weekly trip to Westbury for refuelling and servicing. No. D829 made test runs to Waterloo on 9th August prior to limited introduction of the class from 17th August. From that date, two more 'Warships' were based at Exmouth Junction for duties through to Waterloo, allowing coverage of three return diagrams departing Exeter at 07.30, 12.30 and 17.54, and returning from Waterloo at 13.00, 19.00 and 01.15 (newspapers).

Type '3' diesel-electric No. D6505, seen here at Waterloo in 1966, was still without a yellow warning panel over five years after it was delivered from the Birmingham Railway Carriage & Wagon Company at Smethwick in April 1960. It was renumbered as No. 33005 in 1974 and withdrawn after a generator flashover and fire in 1987. In the background is the Shell Centre, which had been completed by the end of 1966.

Two '4-SUB' units at Waterloo in 1966. On the left is 1951-built No. 4748 and on the right 1949-built No. 4669, working a Waterloo to Kingston via Richmond service. The plain green livery of both units is now relieved by small yellow warning panels.

Maroon No. D806 *Cambrian* and blue BRC&W Co. Type '3' No. D6538 in a photograph taken after January 1968, when the 'Warship' emerged from Swindon Works with full yellow ends. No. D6538 had been fitted in 1967 with equipment for push-pull working from Bournemouth to Weymouth, becoming a Class '33/1' under TOPS, it was renumbered as No. 33118 in 1973 and worked for a further twenty years. 'Warship' operation into Waterloo was scheduled to finish with the semi-fast service to Exeter handed over to Class '33's on 4th October 1971. The latter had been deputising for them on this route for some time, with failures due to broken springs a common problem.

CHAPTER 8 - WATERLOO

For a few years in the 1960s, diesel, steam and electric could be seen side-by-side at Waterloo. In 1967, '4-COR' No. 3147 is in overall blue livery with a small yellow panel on the lower part of the corridor connection, contrasting with the filthy BR Standard 2-6-4T, while a maroon 'Warship' is just visible in the sidings on the left. Petrofina House, in the left background and very near to the Shell Centre, was the London office of Belgian petroleum company, Petrofina SA, which merged with the French oil company Total in 1999 to create Totalfina; its petrol was marketed in the UK under the brand name Fina.

Although slightly outside our twenty-five year period, this picture displays the intricate ironwork supporting the station roof, which was fitted with over 1,000 tons of glass. The now-ubiquitous BRUTEs had taken over what remained of the parcels traffic. In the platform is '2-SAP' No. 5911, which was one of forty-nine units converted in 1974 from the later series of '2-HAP', for Second Class-only services to Weybridge and Windsor because of a severe shortage of suburban stock; most were converted back to their original configuration with First and Second Class seating in 1979-80.

9 – Vauxhall and Battersea L&SWR

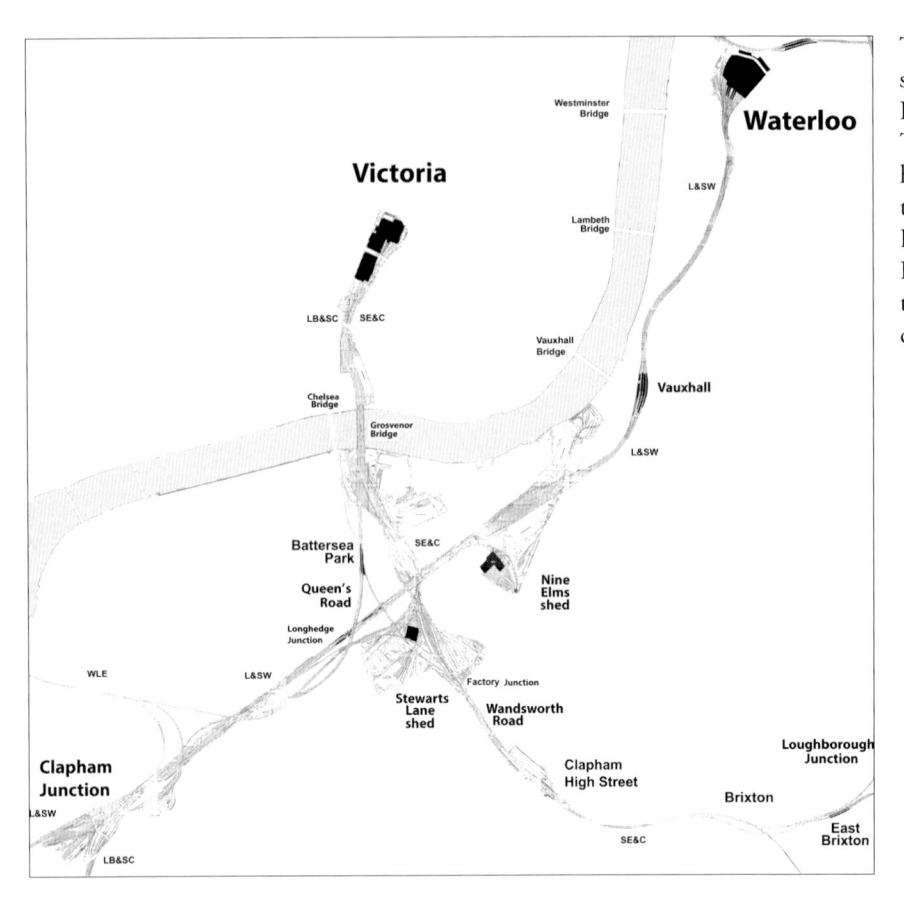

The main lines from Victoria and Waterloo started on opposite sides of the river, with the LB&SCR/SE&CR routes crossing over the Thames on Grosvenor Bridge. Both routes had stations within a short distance of the terminus, at Vauxhall and Queen's Road Battersea on the L&SWR line, and at Battersea Park on the LB&SCR route. The LB&SCR then met the L&SWR at Longhedge Junction, continuing on towards Clapham Junction.

Below: 'N15X' 4-6-0 No. 32327 *Trevithick* between Waterloo and Vauxhall, just beyond West Crossing, with a '4-COR' passing in the opposite direction. The locomotive was rebuilt by the Southern Railway in April 1935 from an LB&SCR Billinton 'L' class 4-6-4T, receiving its BR number in July 1948.

Vauxhall

Ex-LB&SCR Billinton 'Atlantic' No. 32421 *South Foreland* passing Vauxhall hauling a rake of former Great Eastern Railway air-braked suburban stock, probably on a special to Farnborough Air Show on 7th July 1950. This engine was being used because the GER coaches were Westinghouse air-braked and could only be operated by a former Brighton engine, the LB&SCR also being an air-braked railway. Note the early telephone boxes on the gantries.

SE&CR 'D' Class 4-4-0 No. 31737 runs Light Engine through Vauxhall in June 1953. After the appointment of Harry Wainwright as Locomotive & Carriage Superintendent of the newly combined railway, the 'D' Class was the second new design introduced after the 'C' Class 0-6-0s. Fifty-one of these locomotives were built between 1901 and 1907, twenty-one at Ashford including No. 31737, with thirty others by four different private builders; all except one survived into the 1950s. No. 31737 was withdrawn in October 1956 and preserved in the National Collection, and is currently at the National Railway Museum in York.

'D15' 4-4-0 No. 30465 with a train from Lymington to Waterloo passing through Vauxhall in 1955. The headcode indicates a Waterloo to Brockenhurst or Bournemouth West service but Lymington summer Saturday trains also used this standard Bournemouth headcode to and from Brockenhurst, the specific three-disc Lymington code being introduced later. Nine Elms employed its 'D15's on these trains because they could turn on the 50ft turntable at Brockenhurst, where the 'D15' came on. Nine Elms subsequently received 'Schools' 4-4-0s for these duties in 1957. Introduced in 1912, the 'D15's were the last L&SWR design of Dugald Drummond and had a rather ungainly appearance, with their plain chimneys and small smokebox doors. No. 30465 was allocated to Nine Elms from June 1954 until October 1955, when it moved to Eastleigh for its last three months in service. Vauxhall station had been partially rebuilt in 1936 with a new island platform, when the Waterloo approaches were re-arranged following the opening of the flyover at Wimbledon.

CHAPTER 9 - VAUXHALL AND BATTERSEA L&SWR

A view almost unrecognisable today, taken from the London end of Vauxhall station with the Houses of Parliament in the background. All of the houses on the left have been cleared and replaced with high-rise buildings. '2-NOL' No. 1842 heads three other two-car sets on a Waterloo-Alton/Portsmouth train in the early 1950s, the first four coaches going to Alton and the rear four to Portsmouth. No. 1842 was one of the two-car, close-coupled sets converted in the mid-1930s from ex-L&SWR steam stock, primarily for suburban work but they also found use on main line services such as this.

'Britannia' No. 70009 *Alfred the Great* spent four months on the Southern Region in 1951, when three Nine Elms 'Light Pacifics' were loaned to the Great Eastern line, before returning to Norwich in October; it was joined by No. 70014 *Iron Duke* which worked on the Western section for three months until it moved to its permanent shed at Stewarts Lane. After working an Institution of Locomotive Engineers special from Waterloo to Southampton on 24th May, No. 70009 first worked the 'Bournemouth Belle' on 6th June. Note the Southern Region style lamp brackets fitted inside the smoke deflectors.

A lovely scene at Vauxhall, with Southern Railway-style concrete lamp posts, lamp shades and targets to the fore, as 'Merchant Navy' No. 35014 *Nederland Line* passes through with an express from Bournemouth to Waterloo in around 1960. No. 35014 had been rebuilt in 1956 and was fitted with AWS in October 1959. After rebuilding it was transferred from Stewarts Lane to Nine Elms, where it stayed until late 1964.

With 'Big Ben' and the Houses of Parliament in the distance, 'S15' 4-6-0 No. 30514 heads in on a Salisbury 'stopper' in 1961, with three parcels vans added at the rear. Apart from its first two years in traffic, it was always allocated to Feltham, from where it was withdrawn in July 1963.

With construction work underway to the left of the railway, 'N' Class 2-6-0 No. 31811 meets a BR 'Standard' Class '5' 4-6-0 on a Waterloo-Bournemouth train. Design of the 'N' Class, with their Belpaire fireboxes, owed much to Swindon, from where the SE&CR had recruited Harry Holcroft, who had been involved in the design of the GWR Class '43XX' 2-6-0s. However, the tenders were very similar to the later Midland Railway tenders, no doubt influenced by the SE&CR's Chief Draughtsman James Clayton, who came from that company. No. 31811 had been built at Ashford in June 1920 and was at Stewarts Lane from Nationalisation until June 1959, when it was transferred to Guildford, from where it was withdrawn in 1965.

In 1959, the Southern Region decided to transfer the names of withdrawn 'King Arthur' 4-6-0s to twenty of its BR 'Standard' Class '5' 4-6-0s, requiring new narrower nameplates to be cast to fit onto the running plate angle. No. 73088 *Joyous Guard* approaches Vauxhall station on a Salisbury 'stopper', comprising a six-coach non-restaurant car set made up from two 3-set 'L's. The locomotive's name, *Joyous Guard*, acquired in May 1961, was originally on 'King Arthur' No. 30741 which had been withdrawn in 1956. No. 73088 had been transferred in September 1958 to Nine Elms from Stewarts Lane, where it had been allocated since new.

The Southern Counties Touring Society organised the 'Southern Counties Enterprise' on 25th August 1963 using L&NER 'A3' 4-6-2, No. 60112 *St. Simon*. The 'Pacific' worked the train from Waterloo via Southampton Central, Bournemouth Central and Poole to Hamworthy Junction, where 'M7' No. 30052 took over to Hamworthy and return. No. 60112 then worked the special to Dorchester, where it was taken by a pair of GWR 'Pannier' tanks to Portland and on to Maiden Newton, before *St. Simon* returned the tour to Waterloo.

The Lens of Sutton Association

Vauxhall station was next to a large creamery and milk bottling plant operated by United Dairies and milk was unloaded from the rail tanks using flexible hoses at the passenger platforms, through a discharge pipe directly from the rail tanks into the creamery. Milk trains arriving in the evening from the West Country were divided at Clapham Junction so they would not block Vauxhall station while unloading there. This was done in Platform 1 – none of the other platforms were or could be used for this purpose. It was on and accessed from the Up Windsor Local and Platform 2 was on the Up Windsor Through. However, when Platform 1 was occupied by a milk train, any Up services approaching Vauxhall on the Up Windsor Local could be switched to the Up Windsor Through, just to the west of Vauxhall station. The two roads then combined into just a single Up Windsor road about 300 yards to the east of Vauxhall and on to Waterloo. At the same point, the Up Main Through split into the Up Main Through – mainly electric – and the Up Main Relief – mainly steam – so maintaining eight roads to the Waterloo throat. After discharging and washing, the empty tanks would then be taken to Waterloo where they would reverse, there being no facilities for doing this at Vauxhall, and return to Clapham Junction to await the other half of the train. Ex-GWR '57XX' Class 0-6-0PT No. 4681 was working the empties back from Waterloo on the Down Windsor Local in May 1962. Built at Swindon in November 1944, it had arrived at Nine Elms from Danygraig in October 1959 and worked from there until March 1963, when it was transferred to Feltham, with a final move to Bristol Barrow Road in the September followed by withdrawal three months later.

Most of the Eastern section steam stock, including all of the 'L1' 4-4-0s, was transferred to Nine Elms in June 1959, after the inauguration of the Kent Coast electrification. The 'L1's were built in 1926 as a modernised version of the SE&CR 'L' Class 4-4-0s, with a side-window cab, an 'N' Class type smokebox and chimney, and a flat-sided tender. No. 31786 had moved from Gillingham and worked until February 1962 on duties such as the 10.45am Waterloo-Woking ECS which it was hauling here during its final month in service.

After they were displaced from their suburban passenger work, the BR 'Standard' 2-6-4Ts took over ECS workings between Waterloo and the carriage sidings at Clapham Junction alongside the smaller 2-6-2Ts. The first two Class '4' tanks had been transferred to Nine Elms in late 1965, with No. 80144 arriving from Eastleigh in February 1966. Its stay there was brief because it was withdrawn three months later, after less than ten years' service.

As mentioned a little earlier, from September 1964, 'Warship' diesel-hydraulics displaced from Paddington-Bristol and Paddington-Plymouth services were used to dieselise the Southern Region Exeter-Salisbury-Waterloo trains, with a regular interval pattern of semi-fasts between Waterloo and Exeter being introduced. Here, No. D806 *Cambrian* heads the 1pm Waterloo-Exeter through Vauxhall, still in its original green livery which it kept until April 1966. As with all of the diesel-hydraulic classes, the lives of the 'Warships' were brief, with No. D809 being withdrawn in Novemver 1972.

Swindon-built 'Warship' No. D807 *Caradoc* passing the now completed tower blocks at Vauxhall with the 11.00 Waterloo-Salisbury on 1st July 1967. By virtue of its early introduction in June 1959 and late survival until September 1972, *Caradoc* held the distinction of recording the highest 'Warship' mileage, over 1.3 million miles at an average of 100,000 a year during its thirteen year career.

When the first diesel locomotives were ordered in 1955 under the British Railways Modernisation Plan, none were planned for the Southern Region. However, by the late 1950s, the Region had put the case for a Type '3' diesel-electric mounted on two two-axle bogies rather than the alternative English Electric Type '3' Co-Co design which was longer and heavier. The proposal was backed by the Civil Engineer, who said that a Bo-Bo with a top speed of 85mph would have much better route availability, and so a design was produced using the BRC&W Type '2' as a basis but with a more powerful 1,550hp Sulzer engine. The locomotives were to be dual air and vacuum braked, a feature not on contemporary locomotives for the other Regions but which was needed to operate with EMU stock. Another first was the provision of electric train heating, instead of the traditional steam-heating which required what soon proved to be very troublesome boilers on other diesel classes. An initial order for forty-five locomotives was placed in December 1957, a further twenty in October 1958, twelve narrow-bodied examples in July 1959 and a final batch of twenty-one in May 1960. The cab front from the Type '2' design was changed to incorporate a two-character headcode panel, the Southern having no requirement for connecting doors when working in multiple. Enthusiasts quickly gave the class the nickname 'Cromptons', arising from their Crompton-Parkinson traction motors. Snowplough-fitted No. D6524, approaching Vauxhall on 3rd April 1963, was built at Smethwick in October 1960, renumbered under TOPS as No. 33016 in 1974 and withdrawn in 1989. It was almost certainly working the 11.30am Waterloo-Bournemouth West, an Eastleigh turn, which was first diesel-hauled in 1963 when steam heating was not required. The train, which has a roof-boarded 'SO' from a Bournemouth '6 dining set D' at the front, was in fact part of a slightly hybrid set, with the 'SO' unusually located outside the other five cars rather than in the middle. It was also hybrid in the sense that it was a Bulleid three-car 'L' set expanded with a British Railways 'RB' and 1st Corridor/Dining Open built specifically for the '6 dining set D's inside the set and the 'SO' outside. The '6 dining set D' vehicles featured bodysides that were extended to cover the solebars, unlike all the other Bulleid vehicles.

Nine Elms

'4-SUB' No. 4280 travelling outbound from Waterloo between Vauxhall and Nine Elms in the 1960s. The Waterloo to Waterloo via Teddington service is on the Down Windsor Through road and the Portsmouth electric from which the photograph was taken is on the Down Main Through. No. 4280, built in 1948, was one of the first '4-SUB' units built with open centre-gangways rather than the traditional compartment vehicles; their underframes and bogies were recovered from withdrawn sets.

Ex-LB&SCR 'E4' 0-6-2T No. 32476 on a Clapham Junction-Waterloo ECS working in March 1957, a month before it was withdrawn from service. The train is passing under Loco Junction signal box, which dated back to 1918. It was closed in June 1974 when Queen's Road signal box took over its duties. The signal gantry on the right is over the goods lines and the track on the extreme left of the photograph leads to other parts of Nine Elms goods yard. The entrance to Nine Elms shed was by the signal gantry in the distance beyond the signal box; the roofline of the new shed is just visible to the left of the gantry. No. 32476 was built in 1898 and originally named *Beeding* after a village near Horsham in Sussex; it had been at Nine Elms since late 1953.

Queen's Road Battersea

'King Arthur' 4-6-0 No. 30457 *Sir Bedivere* passing through Queen's Road Battersea, having just left Nine Elms yard with a down freight in 1957. The no. 28 on the disc is the locomotive roster number. Built at Eastleigh in April 1925, No. 30457 was one of the first Maunsell 'King Arthur's which were nominally rebuilds of L&SWR Drummond 'G14' and 'P14' 4-6-0s, although they retained little more than the 'water cart' tenders. It was at Nine Elms between June 1951 and October 1957. From March 1955, it was paired with an ex-'H15' 5,200 gallon tender, which was taller and narrower than the standard 5,000 gallon bogie tender. The large advertising board shows Sunday Excursions from Liverpool Street to a variety of destinations in East Anglia, at prices ranging from 9/9 to 15/9. The station was renamed Queenstown Road (Battersea) in May 1980.

'Warship' No. D806 *Cambrian* passes through Queen's Road Battersea with the 17.54 Waterloo-Exeter in March 1967. It had been repainted in maroon with small yellow panels in June 1966. No's D800-812 originally had GWR-style frames built into the nose doors to carry the train reporting numbers but, from No. D813 onwards, the nose doors had four-digit route indicator panels and the earlier locomotives were gradually brought into line at Intermediate overhauls, with No. D806 modified in October 1963. The Decca building, formerly Hampton's Depository, opposite Stewarts Lane shed and in the background above *Cambrian*, shows how close the L&SWR main line was to the SE&CR/LB&SCR lines out of Victoria.

On the same day as above, No. D829 *Magpie* runs light through Queen's Road. It had been in maroon since December 1965, with full yellow ends being added in June 1968. An abortive attempt was made to preserve No. D829 by its namesake ITV childrens' programme in October 1972, after its second withdrawal; the first had been reversed when it was reinstated along with two classmates in early 1972. The South London Line crossed over the L&SWR main line on the viaduct and bridge in front of the Decca building.

10 – Nine Elms

Nine Elms was the principal locomotive depot of the L&SWR and the first engine shed on the site was built in the 1840s. The first part of the modern depot, a large fifteen-road, brick-built, single-ended shed was brought into use around 1889. Further rebuilding before the First World War saw a ten-road extension, known as the 'new shed', constructed alongside the 'old' shed and a new 65ft turntable, with all twenty-five roads leading off it. In the final months of its existence, the L&SWR began construction of a 400-ton ferro-concrete coaling plant, which came into use soon after the 1923 Grouping. There was little change during the Southern Railway years, except for the building of a water softener in around 1930 and an engine washing plant in 1936. During the Second World War, the depot was frequently bombed and sustained severe damage, especially to the roof. Afterwards, it was repaired using asbestos sheeting but much of the original 'old shed' roof was never replaced and the remainder was torn down in the final years.

The shed's allocation was primarily express and mixed traffic engines, together with tank engines used mainly on ECS working in and out of Waterloo, with only a handful of freight locomotives. In SR days there were over twenty 'King Arthur' and 'Lord Nelson' engines and a similar number of mixed traffic 4-6-0s, 'H15's and 'S15's, plus twenty-eight 'M7' 0-4-4Ts on the shed's books in 1933. By the end of the 1940s, the Bulleid 'Pacifics' had arrived with a sizeable allocation of eleven 'Merchant Navy' and six 'Light Pacifics', although the mixed traffic 4-6-0s and 'M7's had both reduced to thirteen.

Ten new BR 'Standard' Class '5' 4-6-0s built at Doncaster, No's 73110-19, arrived in late 1955, allowing the withdrawal of a number of the 'King Arthur's and 'N15X' 'Remembrance' 4-6-0s. In that year, Nine Elms had fifteen 'M7' 0-4-4Ts covering ten ECS duties. They were also used for shunting at Waterloo and at Clapham Yard but this work was mainly carried out by six LB&SCR 'E4' 0-6-2Ts. There was an unexpected change in early 1959 when six ex-GWR 'Pannier' tanks, surplus on their home territory, were transferred from South Wales for the ECS work; they were later joined by another three examples.

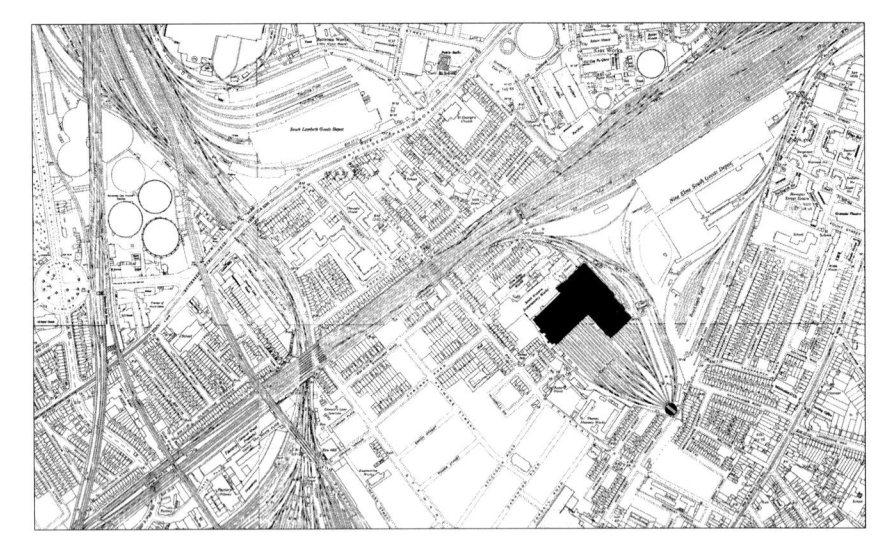

Over 100 engines displaced by the Kent Coast electrification were transferred to Nine Elms in June 1959 from the South Eastern section. These included all of the 'E1', 'L' and 'L1' 4-4-0s and 'R1' 0-6-0Ts, together with twenty-five 'C' 0-6-0s, nine 'D1' 4-4-0s, seven 'H' 0-4-4Ts, two 'O1' 0-6-0s, nine 'Schools' and three 'Merchant Navy's. Many of these went straight into store. All of the South Eastern 'King Arthurs' were moved from Stewarts Lane along with nine of its BR Standard Class '5' 4-6-0s, which took over most of the passenger work previously done by the ageing 'H15' 4-6-0s.

The allocation at the end of 1961 included only eight 'M7's, supported by six 'Pannier's. The 'King Arthurs' and 'Lord Nelsons' had all gone but there were now ten 'Schools' supplementing twenty 'Light Pacifics', twelve 'Merchant Navy's and nineteen BR Class '5' 4-6-0s. The remaining 'M7's and 'Pannier's were all withdrawn or transferred away by 1963, as BR Standard 2-6-2Ts and 2-6-4Ts made redundant by dieselisation and electrification elsewhere on the Region took over the ECS work from the end of 1962.

Nine Elms survived to the bitter end of steam working on the Southern in July 1967 but in its final years became effectively a servicing point. Probably as a result of growing labour shortages in the capital, in August 1964 its 'Pacifics' and half of its BR Class '5' 4-6-0s were transferred away, the remainder following in 1965. Since they were now allocated for maintenance to Eastleigh, Bournemouth, Salisbury and Weymouth, Nine Elms became the place where they were merely turned, coaled and sent back after working in to Waterloo. Four 'Light Pacifics' came back in January 1965, joined by eight more in June 1966 and the remaining 'Merchant Navy's also returned, in April 1967, to join the 2-6-2Ts and 2-6-4Ts, and most stayed until the very end.

The sign says it all as 'West Country' No. 34034 *Honiton* attracts attention while it turns. *Honiton* was rebuilt in 1960 and allocated to Nine Elms from June 1966 until withdrawn the following July. The blocks of flats were completed in 1955.

CHAPTER 10 - NINE ELMS

The shed was reached by a back-shunt from a terminal spur on the Down side at Loco Junction near Queen's Road. This was connected by crossover with all eight running lines into Waterloo, although most Light Engines used the Up Main Through and Down Main Local lines. It was the last operational steam shed in the capital, closing on 9th July 1967 and all traces soon disappeared under the New Covent Garden wholesale fruit, vegetable and flower market development, which opened on the site in 1974.

1950s

'Merchant Navy' No. 35027 *Port Line* at Nine Elms in 1949, in malachite green with no tender lettering and awaiting its naming ceremony, with the nameplate concealed by a purpose made wooden cover. It was completed at Eastleigh in December 1948 and the naming ceremony was not until 24th April 1950 at Southampton Docks, for which it was specially called in to works to be repainted in BR blue. No. 35027 was rebuilt in 1957 and was rescued from Barry for preservation in 1982. After restoration, it spent over a decade on the Bluebell Railway before moving to Swanage. It is currently awaiting a major overhaul to bring it back to main line condition. By 1949, Nine Elms had eleven 'Merchant Navy's (Exmouth Junction had seven, and Salisbury and Bournemouth six each); it subsequently acquired another, bringing the total to twelve by November 1954.

It is just about possible to see that No. 32328 *Hackworth* was in green livery with BRITISH RAILWAYS in full on the tender. It was one of seven 'N15X' 4-6-0s rebuilt from 4-6-4Ts in the mid-1930s and all were named after distinguished 19th Century railway engineers. Renumbered in October 1948, *Hackworth* was allocated to Basingstoke from Southern Railway days until withdrawn in January 1955, the first of the class to go, because of badly cracked frames and a weakened firebox crown.

Immediately before the First World War, the LB&SCR built two 'L' class 4-6-4Ts, followed by a further five in 1921-22. When the last one entered traffic, it was named *Remembrance* as the company's War Memorial engine, carrying a plaque inscribed '*In grateful remembrance of the 532 men of the L.B.& S.C.Rly. who gave their lives for their country, 1914-1919*'. In 1934, Maunsell began re-building the engines as Class 'N15X' 4-6-0s, using the same boilers, smokeboxes and fireboxes, and were paired with standard Urie L&SWR tenders. They were mainly used on secondary duties such as the Bournemouth and Salisbury semi-fasts and milk trains, and after the Second World War they were all allocated to Basingstoke. The fireman of No. 32333 *Remembrance* was up on the tender, trimming the coal which had just been loaded on from the Nine Elms coaling plant. The engine, still in Southern Railway green livery here, although it had been renumbered in May 1948, was withdrawn in April 1956.

Ex-LB&SCR Billinton 'E4' 0-6-2T No. 32500, originally named *Puttenham*, at Nine Elms next to 'M7' 0-4-4T No. 30241 on 25th May 1952. It was allocated to Nine Elms from November 1948 until withdrawn in January 1962. The 'E4' radial tanks were used mainly on shunting work but also helped out the 'M7's on ECS movements.

Fully coaled up with what appears to be a load mainly consisting of slack, 'King Arthur' No. 30455 *Sir Launcelot* stands on the roads of the 'old' shed on 14th March 1953. It was one of the 1925-built Maunsell engines with a Drummond 4,000 gallon 'watercart' tender, with inside axleboxes and the small version of the first BR emblem. No. 30455 spent its career on the Western section, transferring to Nine Elms from Salisbury in June 1952; it left for Basingstoke in October 1957 and was withdrawn in April 1959. Note the small curved splasher-like feature immediately above the leading driving wheels, which was a hinged cover to facilitate inspection and lubrication of the junction of the pivot, radius rod and expansion link – a distinctive Maunsell feature. The letter 'A' below the stock number was the old Southern Railway power classification which used to be on the valence/running plate just before the drop/curve down to the buffer beam; they were discontinued when the British Railways power classifications were introduced.

The Drummond '700' Class 0-6-0s shared many standard parts, including the boiler, firebox, cylinders and motion, with the 'M7' 0-4-4Ts and other contemporary L&SWR classes. Although superheated during the 1920s, they were displaced in Southern Railway days by the advent of the 'S15' 4-6-0s and the 'Q' 0-6-0s, which relegated the class to secondary duties. No. 30346 was built by Dübs & Co. in 1897 and was a visitor from Feltham, where it had been allocated since April 1948.

Drummond '700' Class 0-6-0 No. 30701, built by Dübs & Co in 1897, shows off its austere lines at Nine Elms on 14th March 1953. The engine was allocated there throughout the period under British Railways, until withdrawn in July 1961.

A photograph taken while No. 30859 *Lord Hood* was allocated to Nine Elms, where it stayed until June 1958. Note the large diameter Lemaître exhaust and the high-sided tender with which it had been paired since 1940. It was unique in having 6ft 3ins driving wheels instead of the 6ft 7ins on the rest of the class, probably in an attempt to assess whether these would be more suitable over the heavily graded lines west of Salisbury or on the Eastern Section.

In a scene typical of Nine Elms in the 1950s, 'Merchant Navy' No. 35018 *British India Line* stands with 'M7' 0-4-4T No. 30241 and 'S15' 4-6-0 No. 30511 all 'chimney into the shed' in June 1959. No. 35018 was the first 'Merchant Navy' to be rebuilt, emerging following a three month reconstruction in February 1956 in a form radically changed from its original design. The class was known for its maintenance difficulties, together with high coal consumption and so the chain driven valve gear, operating between the frames and running within a sealed oil 'bath' and a constant source of trouble, was replaced by conventional Walschaerts gear. Although the term oil 'bath' is commonly used, it was actually an oil sump, much the same as in most motor cars. The motion did not actually run in the oil but was pressure-lubricated from it and then the oil drained back into the sump, again like a car. In its latter days, the gear was not particularly unreliable but was difficult and unpleasant, and hence expensive, to repair when it did need attention.

1960s

The residents in those flats had a grandstand view of the turntable but they would have been very pleased to see the end of steam. The 70ft under-girder turntable which replaced the previous 65ft over-girder table in the mid-1950s, was the critical point of the depot. Engines either turned straight after coaling or were directed to one of the twenty-five shed roads for stabling until their next duty, or for attention. 'M7' 0-4-4T No. 30039 was on Nine Elms roster 53 on 28th April 1962. Built here in 1898 as one of the short framed 'M7s' with the front sandboxes on the splashers, it was also originally allocated here until 1937, when it moved to Exmouth Junction. It still wears a 71A Eastleigh shedplate although it left there to return to the capital in March 1960; withdrawal occurred in March 1963. In 1955, Nine Elms had fifteen 'M7' 0-4-4Ts on its books covering ten ECS duties; they were also used for shunting at Waterloo and at Clapham Yard.

CHAPTER 10 - NINE ELMS

The L&SWR began construction of a 400 ton ferro-concrete mechanical coaling plant at Nine Elms which came into use soon after the 1923 grouping and spanned two of the approach roads to the shed. 'West Country' 34031 *Torrington* has just filled its tender and is ready to move off. Rebuilt at the end of 1958, Torrington was transferred to Nine Elms in March 1959 from Exmouth Junction. Its AWS and speedometer were fitted in June 1960. Probably as a result of growing labour shortages in the Capital, in August 1964 all of the Nine Elms Pacifics were transferred away, with Torrington going to Eastleigh, although a number returned over the next three years. Maintenance responsibility passed to Eastleigh, Bournemouth, Salisbury and Weymouth, and Nine Elms was reduced to the place where they were merely turned and coaled, and sent back after working in to Waterloo. No. 34031 was an early withdrawal for a rebuilt 'Light' Pacific, in February 1965.

Drummond '700' Class 'Black Motor' 0-6-0 No. 30699 of 1897 vintage was allocated to Nine Elms throughout the 1950s until withdrawn in July 1961.

By way of a contrast with the Victorian outline of the '700' Class 0-6-0s, we have the severe functional form of the Bulleid 'Q1' 0-6-0s. No. 33009, photographed at Nine Elms in 1961, spent over a decade at Feltham, from May 1953 until September 1964. The engine was fitted with AWS and the steam reverser, which looks like two conjoined cylinders, can be seen above the centre driving wheel.

Ex-LB&SCR Billinton 'E2' 0-6-0T No. 32102 at Nine Elms on 18th August 1961. It was one of the last two of the eight members of the ten-strong class to remain at Stewarts Lane, moving away to join several classmates on Southampton Docks shed's books, although there must be some doubt as to whether it ever left London since it was withdrawn in October 1961. The bunker back has an over plate repair and some wag has chalked 'Scrap' on the side tank.

Ex-LB&SCR Billinton 'E4' 0-6-2T No. 32487 at Nine Elms in around 1962. Note the long power classification '2P 2FB', a unique Southern Region touch. Unlike other Regions, they decided to sub-divide the freight power classes '2' and '5' into 'A' and 'B' groups, 'A' being used for the classes with a higher braking ability. Therefore, where a tank engine such as the 'E4' had the same tractive effort as a tender engine, in this case the 'C2X' 0-6-0, the tank was given the 'B' suffix because of its inferior braking ability. It was fitted with a Westinghouse brake and the top double-acting steam piston on the cab side is in terrible condition. It drove the bottom double-acting air piston and often had the attention of the coal hammer before it started working. When built in 1899, No. 32487 carried the name *Fishergate*, a place near Brighton and the engine was shedded at Nine Elms from December 1957 until withdrawn at the end of December 1962. Nine Elms' large stud of 'M7' 0-4-4Ts covered most ECS duties between Waterloo and Clapham Junction but the 'E4's were also used on this work, although they were mainly employed on shunting at Waterloo and at Clapham Yard.

The 'L1' 4-4-0s from the Eastern section spent a short time before withdrawal at Nine Elms, after they were ousted from their traditional territory in June 1959 when the Kent Coast electrification went live. No. 31786, outside the 'old' shed on 18th August 1961, had been transferred from Gillingham and was withdrawn in February 1962.

The Western Region had a surfeit of 0-6-0 'Pannier' tanks at the end of the 1950s and it was decided to transfer some of them to the Southern Region, to replace ageing pre-Group types. Six went to Dover and six to Nine Elms in January 1959, including Class '57XX' No. 4672 from Cardiff Cathays; they were later joined at Nine Elms by another three 'Pannier's. No. 4672, one of three on shed, remained at Nine Elms until March 1963 when it moved to Feltham. Note the additional two Southern-type lamp irons on the back of the bunker to accommodate the discs carried by all the Region's steam engines; the other four brackets have also been changed from the Western Region type.

CHAPTER 10 - NINE ELMS

'Lord Nelson' No. 30862 *Lord Collingwood* stands outside the 'new' shed and in front of the mechanical coaling plant on 28th April 1962. It was built in 1929 and allocated to Eastleigh from June 1956 until withdrawn in October 1962, accummulating the highest recorded mileage for the class, of 1,390,329 miles. The Lemaître exhaust and large diameter chimney were applied to all of the class members in 1939, whilst all had also been paired with 5,000 gallon bogie tenders in 1932; these were originally flat-sided but from 1937 the sides were increased in height with turned-in tops and self-trimming bunkers. The speedometer and AWS were fitted in May 1961.

No. 35028 *Clan Line* has just come on to the shed from Loco Junction and is moving towards the coaling stage on 28th April 1962. Built by British Railways at Eastleigh in December 1948 and rebuilt at the end of 1959, it was the first 'Merchant Navy' to be preserved when purchased by the Merchant Navy Locomotive Preservation Society (MNLPS) from British Railways in August 1967. When first acquired, it was housed at the Longmoor Military Railway, the army railway training base in Hampshire. Unfortunately, the Ministry of Defence decided the railway would close in 1969 and *Clan Line* had to be moved, initially to a site a few miles away at Liss and then again to a privately-owned base at Ashford in Kent. When British Rail lifted the ban on the operation of privately owned steam locomotives, *Clan Line* was one of the first preserved locomotives to participate and, in April 1974, operated its first main line steam tour from Basingstoke to Westbury and return. In 1975, it moved to the Bulmer's Cider Railway Centre at Hereford, from where it continued to operate on the main line, although there were several more changes of base over the next two decades. In 1994, Venice Simplon Orient Express (VSOE) hired the engine to haul its luxury Pullman train from Victoria to Portsmouth Harbour and return. This was a great success and so VSOE decided to introduce steam haulage on a number of its services. Thus began a long association of *Clan Line* with the now 'British Pullman' train, which continues today with around twenty excursions every year. This also provided an opportunity to base it at the railway maintenance facility at Stewarts Lane, and the engine, support coach and back-up workshop facilities were moved there in March 1999, and established in the former electric locomotive maintenance building. Stewarts Lane, where the engine had been allocated between 1950 and 1959, remains the MNLPS base to this day. *Clan Line* has recently completed a major overhaul at Crewe and has now returned to VSOE operation there.

CHAPTER 10 - NINE ELMS

When the Southern Railway needed more goods engines in the Second World War, instead of building more of the recently introduced 'Q' Class 0-6-0s, the newly installed Chief Mechanical Engineer, Oliver Bulleid, chose to build an 0-6-0 freight engine, the 'Q1', to a fundamentally different design. It had much in common with his 'Merchant Navy' 'Pacifics', such as Bulleid Firth Brown Boxpox wheel centres, multiple jet exhaust and stovepipe chimneys but, surprisingly had inside Stephenson valve gear, although the cylinder and valve arrangement was entirely conventional and based on the 'Q' Class. Both classes had outside admission valves giving very direct exhaust passages to the blastpipe. However, what really set the engine apart was its radical appearance. In order to keep the weight down and make efficient use of materials, there was no conventional running plate or splashers to hinder access to the inside motion. The boiler was lagged with a product called 'Idaglass', used because of the wartime shortage of asbestos; conventional cladding was replaced by thin sheets which followed the contours of the boiler, firebox and smokebox. The firebox grate area was almost twenty-five per cent higher than that of the 'Q' and the firebox heating surface was almost half as big again, yet the weight was only 1³/₄ tons more. The resulting engine had a tractive effort of 30,000lbs, compared to the 'Q' at 26,157lbs, and its relatively low weight allowed it to operate over ninety-three per cent of the Southern system. Their 3,700 gallon tenders were equally lightweight although, within a few years, they were weighted down with concrete to assist braking and stability. The man with his head inside the frames of No. 33028 at Nine Elms on 28th April 1962 is the driver, demonstrating the ease of access to the inside motion. The engine was built at Brighton in July 1942 and had been allocated to Feltham since October 1948; AWS had been fitted, with the cylinder visible under the cab.

Unrebuilt 'West Country' No. 34002 *Salisbury* in front of the 'old' shed on 28th April 1962. The 1945-built engine was at Exmouth Junction from new until September 1964, when it was transferred to Eastleigh, before quickly moving on to Nine Elms in January 1965, where it remained until withdrawal. The AWS and speedometer were fitted in June 1960.

The contrast in appearance between the original Bulleid 'Pacifics' and the rebuilt engines was as great as their mechanical difference, with the chain driven motion enclosed in an oil bath replaced by conventional Walschaerts valve gear as previously mentioned. No. 34004 *Yeovil* had been rebuilt in 1958; it was transferred from Stewarts Lane to Eastleigh in May 1961 and in October 1965 to Bournemouth. The condition of the paintwork suggests this picture was taken shortly after completion of a General Overhaul at the end of 1963.

The end

Nine Elms survived to the bitter end of steam working on the Southern in July 1967 but mainly as a servicing point in its final years. The weed-covered tracks contain only a few filthy, run-down BR 'Standards' and 'Pacifics', many out of use, as Battersea power station belches out smoke in the background.

A view taken in 1967, probably after the end of Southern steam on 9th July, with No. 34008 *Padstow* devoid of its name and number plates alongside two BR 'Standards' awaiting their fate, which had also lost their smokebox plates. The 'West Country' had been allocated to Nine Elms from June 1966 until withdrawn.

11 – Clapham Junction

Clapham Junction was eloquently described in the *Railway Wonders of the World* in 1938, and most of this held true until the end of Southern Region steam in 1967:

'It has been said, in a phrase that has become proverbial, that everyone one meets, sooner or later, under the clock of Charing Cross Station. Of another Southern Railway station – Clapham Junction – it may be said that eventually everyone passes through it. Clapham Junction retains many distinctions even in an age in which the records of to-day become the commonplaces of to-morrow. It handles more passenger trains a day than any other station in the British Isles. It is, taking all factors into account, entitled to call itself one of the world's busiest railway stations. It is a focal point for the largest and busiest suburban electric railway traffic in the world, besides forming one of the gateways to Europe, America, and the East.

It adds to its other activities that of serving as one of the main transfer and interchange points for passenger and goods traffic passing between the main railway systems north and south of the Thames. Its name has naturally, therefore, become synonymous with that of a busy meeting-place. By one of the many curiosities of English railway geography, Clapham Junction is not situated in Clapham, but in the adjoining suburb of Battersea. The London and South Western Railway owned at one time a passenger station officially known as Wandsworth, which also was in Battersea. This structure was eventually replaced by a station to which it had originally been intended to give the name of Battersea Junction. The reason for the change of name 'is a mystery', says one historian, 'unless we accept the usual explanation that it sounded more important, for it is very much in Battersea, and over a mile from Clapham, to which a branch was never proposed'. It is not quite clear at this date why Clapham should 'sound more important' than Battersea; but, whatever the explanation, the fact remains that the name of one of the most famous railway stations in the world is based on an error in geography.

To understand why Clapham Junction should hold the record for passenger train movements, it is necessary to understand something of the history and geography of the railways south of the Thames, and of the special conditions existing on those lines, as far as short distance traffic is concerned. As well as dealing with the traffic of 'foreign' companies, Clapham Junction serves both the Western (London and South-Western) and Central (London, Brighton and South Coast) Sections of the Southern Railway. Every train entering and leaving Waterloo Station – the busiest passenger terminus in the country – has to pass through the junction.

The main reason for the exceptionally heavy traffic movements at both Victoria and Waterloo is that the Southern Railway is predominantly a passenger-carrying system. There is no parallel to the immense suburban network within a radius of twenty-five miles of its numerous London terminal stations. The reason is that an exceptionally large proportion of the Southern's total route mileage of 2,186 lies within this small area. The whole of the long- and short-distance passenger traffic in and out of Waterloo has to pass through Clapham Junction, which also handles much of the Brighton line traffic, including the majority of the sixty minutes non-stop expresses between London and Brighton. In addition, the station serves the West London Extension Railway, which affords a through route linking up the Southern main line with those of the Great Western and LMS Railways. It handles also a vast amount of interchange traffic in goods and parcels, and serves as well as a marshalling and assembling depot. The traffic density and strategical importance of the junction thus become intelligible. Clapham Junction has seventeen platforms [all except two of which were through lines] and two through roads, without counting those used for shunting and other purposes.

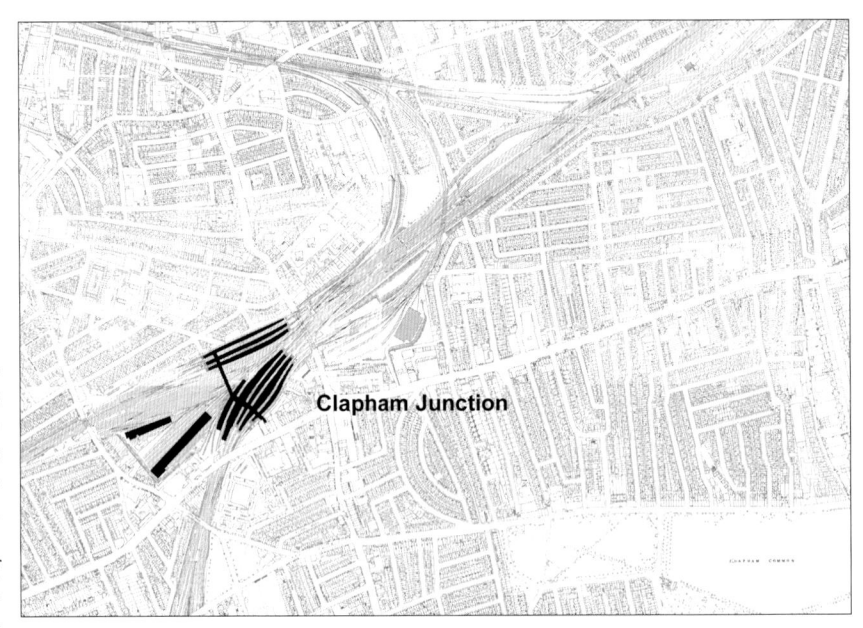

The Brighton line did not reach the site of Clapham Junction until many years after the London and South Western. The original Brighton line terminus was at London Bridge, and Victoria Station was not opened until 1860, although a line between London and Brighton was in use throughout as early as 1841. The third Partner, so to speak, in Clapham Junction is the West London Extension Railway. This line, which is five miles in length, is jointly owned by the Great Western, LMS, and Southern Railways. It extends from Clapham Junction to Kensington (Addison Road), where it links up with the two and a quarter miles long West London Railway, which is the joint property of the Great Western and LMS Railways. The combined system, insignificant though it is in point of mileage, occupies a position of importance on the British railway traffic map, since it connects the Southern Railway with the LMS (via Willesden Junction), and also links up with the Great Western main line.

The peak periods are from 8 to 10 am and from 5 to 7 pm (except on Saturdays). It is during those hours that Clapham Junction assumes its most striking aspect, since the immense volume of suburban traffic is swollen by the important long-distance residential business, such as that between London and Brighton and Worthing. As heavy loading is the rule, it has been estimated that during the rush hours at least two thousand people pass through the station every minute. There is no minute during the twenty-four hours during which Clapham Junction is not kept busy. Empty passenger trains are assembled; shunting and light engine movements are in progress.

It is doubtful whether the vast majority of the travellers who pass through Clapham Junction every working day of their lives ever realize the great size of the station. This is remarkably deceptive, partly because of the somewhat fan-shaped lay-out, and partly because the roofs are of the veranda pattern, and thus lack the imposing appearance of an overall covering. Clapham Junction was opened on March 2, 1863, and was from the beginning the joint property of the London, Brighton and South Coast, and London and South Western Companies. [Each company including the West London Extension had its own platforms and booking office]. The total area enclosed by its platforms is twenty-four and a quarter acres; it has also about ten and a half acres of sidings.'

CHAPTER 11 - CLAPHAM JUNCTION

Opposite Page Left: Clapham Junction is in the lower left corner of the map. The Brighton lines are at the bottom edge, the West of England main lines in the centre, and at the top, the Windsor and Reading tracks. The main West of England and Windsor lines diverge at the Waterloo end of the platforms, the carriage yard being located between the two, whereas the Brighton and West of England tracks diverge a short distance from the country end of the station. Curving away to the top left, with access to both the L&SWR and L&BSCR side of the junction, is the West London Extension Railway, which was five miles in length, and from 1923 was jointly owned by the Great Western, LM&SR and Southern Railways. It extended from Clapham Junction to Kensington (Addison Road), where it linked up with the 2¼ miles long West London Railway, which was the joint property of the Great Western and LM&S railways. The terminal approach to Waterloo, by way of Vauxhall and Queen's Road (Battersea) stations, is by eight tracks as far as West London Junction, where the lines fan out to serve Clapham Junction.

1950s

In a far cry from its heyday on the SE&CR, 'D' class 4-4-0 No. 31737 had been reduced to local freight work by January 1952. It had been stored several times in the previous year on the Eastern section but had been transferred to the ex-SE&CR shed at Reading in early 1951. No. 31737 was withdrawn in October 1956 and preserved in the National Collection and is now at York Museum. The carriage washing plant which cleaned the empty stock as it came out of Waterloo to the Clapham Junction sidings is just visible in the distance.

Another 'D' Class 4-4-0 also transferred from the Eastern section to Reading in early 1951 was No. 31746 which was employed on Waterloo to Clapham Junction ECS duty in February 1952.

Built for the L&SWR by Dübs & Co. in 1899, Class 'T9' 4-4-0 No. 30719 was on Duty '56' with milk empties for the West Country. It was allocated to Nine Elms from December 1950 until October 1952, when it moved away to Salisbury.

'Lord Nelson' No. 30864 *Sir Martin Frobisher* on a Bournemouth express in the mid-1950s, with the first five coaches in 'blood and custard' livery and the last three in green. The 'Nelsons' were only ever allocated to a few sheds: Stewarts Lane or Nine Elms from new and then variously at these two sheds until, at the end of the war, some went to Bournemouth and all of them finally ended up at Eastleigh. No. 30864 was at Bournemouth from October 1954 until November 1959. Clapham Junction 'A' signal box is behind the engine and the carriage washing plant is to the right of the last coach.

The two LM&SR-designed diesel-electrics handled some of the Southern Region's most prestigious trains for a short time in 1953 and early 1954. The second of these, No. 10001, which had been transferred from the London Midland Region in April 1953, was passing through Clapham Junction with the Down 'Bournemouth Belle' Pullman on 21st March 1954.

Nearing the end of its journey, 'Merchant Navy' No. 35012 *United States Line* passes through with an express from Bournemouth, also on 21st March 1954. The locomotive had been transferred from Nine Elms to Bournemouth for three months in February 1954. Its tender had been modified and the front casing ahead of the cylinders removed during a General Overhaul completed in July 1952 and it was rebuilt in 1957.

Nine Elms shed had around half a dozen ex-LB&SCR 'E4' 0-6-2Ts on its allocation throughout the 1950s. They were mainly employed on shunting duties at Clapham Junction, although they did share some of the ECS work with the 'M7' 0-4-4Ts. No. 32486 is here paired with one of the two shunter's trucks used in Clapham carriage sidings as it moves an SR bogie utility van. These vehicles were converted in 1931, utilising the frames of ex-L&SWR Adams 'A12' Class engine tenders. No. 32486 was at Nine Elms until withdrawn in January 1959; the shunter's trucks fared little better and when the diesel shunters came they were taken out of use, although one re-appeared at Exmouth Junction for a time.

'E4' radial 0-6-2T No. 32497 also with a shunter's truck at Clapham Junction in 1953. The engine was at Nine Elms until withdrawal in November 1959

This is a former L&SWR 'Motor Set', rebuilt initially on 62ft long underframes and then further modified as a '4-SUB'. Set No. 4135, which had been augmented by an ex-L&SWR ten-compartment trailer, was photographed on a Waterloo to Waterloo via New Malden and Kingston service at Clapham Junction on 24th January 1954.

Set No. 4226, another former L&SWR 'Motor Set' rebuilt initially on 62ft long underframes and then further augmented by the addition of an ex-L&SWR ten-compartment into a '4-SUB', was on a Waterloo to Chessington service at Clapham Junction just a week earlier, on 17th January. It is crossing from the Down Main Through to the Down Main Local. Clapham Junction 'B' signal box on the right was opened in October 1952, when colour light signalling came into operation on the ex-LB&SCR lines, replacing four former LB&SCR boxes: Clapham Junction 'B' and 'C', New Wandsworth and Pouparts Junction, where the high- and low-level lines to Victoria diverged. The box, which had a 103-lever frame and controlled the lines from Victoria, was in use until 1980, when Victoria Signalling Centre took over the area.

'4-SUB' No. 4344 at Clapham Junction working the 11.33am Victoria-Balham-Streatham Hill-West Croydon-St. Helier-Wimbledon-Tulse Hill-Holborn Viaduct service on 31st October 1954. This had also been converted from a three-car '1496' Class in 1946 but using a ten-compartment, six-a-side, steel panelled trailer, the different outline of which shows it as the third vehicle in the set. The headcode should be 'P' with a 'bar' over the top rather than a 'dot'; the headcode as shown had no application here, although it could have applied for the Wimbledon-Tulse Hill-Blackfriars portion but not to Holborn Viaduct, so the motorman may have just been avoiding the need to change it at Wimbledon. *The Lens of Sutton Association*

When British Railways began to introduce new multiple unit stock in the early 1950s, they differed in appearance from the earlier Southern Railway designs with flat cab fronts and body sides instead of the 'V' fronted, panelled stock. The 1951 design of four-coach suburban sets were built at Eastleigh with English Electric traction equipment and electro-pneumatic brakes. The motorman's compartment was entered from the guard's compartment and had sliding side windows. There were roller-blind route indicators and buck-eye automatic couplers at the outer ends. The control cables and brake hoses were placed so that coupling and uncoupling could be carried out without the need to go between the coaches at ground level. '4-EPB' No. S5105 was working a circular Waterloo to Waterloo via Richmond and Brentford service in 1954. It has the 1949 version of the BR livery, with an 'S'-prefixed unit number on the front end that was later dispensed with, an 'S' before and after the vehicle number, and 'lion & wheel' crests. Also, the unit has a 'bus line' connection at the front end, which was used to connect together all current pick-up shoes on multi-unit trains. This was later removed, so that the facility applied only within each individual set to avoid 'gapping'.

CHAPTER 11 - CLAPHAM JUNCTION

An early '4-EPB', No. S5013 built in 1952, passes under Clapham Junction 'A' signal box, with a circular Waterloo to Waterloo service via Brentford and Richmond on 21st March 1954. The four-aspect colour light signalling had only been in operation on the 'Brighton' side of the Junction since late 1952, whereas the Waterloo lines had been colour light controlled since the 1936 re-signalling.

A spotter watches the race between a 'King Arthur' 4-6-0 and an EMU on the ex-L&SWR Down Main Local with a Waterloo-Shepperton service on 21st March 1954. Both 'A' and 'B' signal boxes are in view.

The first '2-BIL' units were built in 1935 for use on semi-fast services. They were close-coupled within set, non-vestibuled, corridor units. with English Electric electrical equipment. They had steel underframes and steel panelled bodies on hardwood frames and further batches were built in 1936, 1937 and 1938. No. 2110, at the front of a Waterloo-Alton/Portsmouth via Earlsfield train, had been built in 1937 for the Portsmouth and Alton routes.

CHAPTER 11 - CLAPHAM JUNCTION

'4-SUB' No. 4550, seen here working a Victoria to Guildford via Mitcham Junction and Epsom service on 27th May 1956, was one of over a hundred '4-SUB's rebuilt from ex-LB&SCR steam or electric stock in the late 1940s. The third vehicle with a different profile is a steel panelled trailer, which was added to the three older vehicles. The service description is correct for the headcode shown, although at that time trains by this route usually terminated at Effingham Junction. The West London Extension line to Kensington curves away on the right of the picture.

Built at Doncaster in November 1956 and allocated to Nine Elms up to August 1964, BR 'Standard' Class '5' 4-6-0 No. 73115 did not receive its *King Pellinore* name until February 1960. It has a 'BR1F' Type 5,625 gallon tender, the largest capacity type, which carried seven tons of coal and was not fitted with water pick-up gear. Note the large 10 inch cab numbers used by Doncaster Works.

The fireman is putting the lamp on, so presumably 'Standard' Class '4' 4-6-0 No. 75042 had just taken over a returning excursion. It was allocated to Bedford from January 1955 until January 1960, when it moved to Leicester.

Clapham Junction 'A' signal box, which controlled the lines from Waterloo, was built in 1912 and originally designated as Clapham Junction East box until 1924. It was carried on two 120ft long, hog-backed girders 30ft apart and connected by steel cross-girders supporting the deck. At 8.36am, during the Monday morning rush hour on 10th May 1965, one end of the box suddenly dropped by about four feet. The 'Six Bells' code was immediately sent to the surrounding boxes and everything came to a grinding halt, with Waterloo closed for the whole day. The box had been fitted with an overall roof made from steel plates weighing 40 tons as an air raid precaution in 1940 and this was probably a contributory factor to the collapse. The Ministry of Transport Inquiry put the blame squarely on the local District Engineer and his staff, having found extensive corrosion in the diagonal support girder which had failed, and others were also in poor condition but when last examined in June 1964 this had not been thought to be serious. The steel roof was quickly removed and the damage repaired, allowing the box to operate for a further twenty-five years until closure in May 1990. With the 'A' box behind it, 'Q1' 0-6-0 No. 33038 was running light through Clapham Junction on 13th June 1956. Built in December 1942, No. 33038 moved between various London area sheds and by February 1955 was based at Nine Elms, where it stayed until February 1961.

A Stanier Class '5' comes off the West London line and climbs towards Platform 17 with an excursion train from the London Midland Region on 27th May 1956. In the left distance are several gas tank wagons parked adjacent to a storage tank. The large advertisement is for Booth's gin and to the left of this is the ex-L&NWR Falcon Lane goods depot, which remained in use until 1968. After the Second World War, only the short section of the West London line between Kensington and Earls Court was reopened for passenger traffic, with the service being provided by London Transport's District Line but only when there was an exhibition at Olympia. A workmen's steam hauled passenger service ran between Clapham Junction and Kensington, with two trains in the morning rush hour and two in the evening, but this service received little promotion and most people were unaware of its existence. The line remained busy with around thirty freight trains in each direction daily, whilst holiday excursions and special cross-country workings were common.

An LM&SR designed Fairburn 2-6-4T No. 42087 at Clapham Junction with a Tunbridge Wells West train on 27th May 1956. Built at Brighton in March 1951, it had been recently transferred to Tunbridge Wells West from its original shed at Brighton.

A Chessington service on 13th June 1956, with No. 4306, a '4-SUB' re-formed in 1945 from an L&SWR '3-SUB' augmented with a steel panelled trailer – the third coach in the picture.

CHAPTER 11 - CLAPHAM JUNCTION

Empty coaching stock (ECS) workings

Only a few of the locomotive hauled trains arriving at Waterloo were turned around to form an outgoing service. The terminus did not have any engine release roads and so incoming engines were trapped. Therefore, most trains were worked out to a holding point at Clapham Yard. In the mid-1950s, there were over thirty workings each way during the winter weekday time table; the summer months and especially Saturdays saw this number increase considerably. The ECS workings were never dieselised, unlike those on the other Regions' London termini.

In 1955, Nine Elms had fifteen 'M7' 0-4-4Ts covering ten duties, No's 50 to 60. They were allowed nine minutes to cover the journey of just less than four miles to Waterloo and ten minutes in the reverse direction, presumably to allow for the stock to pass through the washing plant. They also carried out shunting at Waterloo and at Clapham Yard but this work was mainly the preserve of half a dozen LB&SCR 'E4' 0-6-2Ts, which worked duties 61 to 63. A few ECS workings were the responsibility of the incoming or outgoing train engines, which meant that they utilised the large 4-6-0s and 'Pacifics'. No. 30322 was a Nine Elms 1900-built short framed 'M7', and was allocated there from 1937 until withdrawn in November 1958. The 'M7's were the staple power for the ECS workings from Waterloo to the extensive carriage sidings at the junction. Clapham Yard was spread over ten acres and had fifty-two carriage roads located in the fork between the West of England and Reading lines, and another seven, known as Kensington sidings, to the north of the Reading line. No. 30322 is in front of the carriage cleaning shed in the centre of the picture, which spanned roads 7 to 11; roads 30 to 32 served a carriage repair shed which is just visible to the right of the 'M7'. Roads No's 1 to 38 were known as Park sidings, and 39-52 as Yard sidings. There was a two-track carriage washing plant situated between the West London Junction and Clapham Junction 'A' signal boxes, although not every carriage set coming from Waterloo would use it.

A few ECS duties were the responsibility of the incoming or outgoing train engines, which meant that they utilised 'Pacifics' and large 4-6-0s such as 'H15' No. 30484. This picture at Clapham Junction was probably taken shortly after a General Overhaul completed in March 1951, given the condition of the paintwork and the original 5,200 gallon bogie tender. It was always allocated to Nine Elms, except for a spell of slightly over four years at Feltham during the war years, and was withdrawn in 1959. Known by enginemen and enthusiasts as 'Chonkers', the 'H15's were Robert Urie's first design for the L&SWR, a mixed traffic, two-cylinder superheated 4-6-0, which had piston valves above the cylinders driven by outside Walschaerts valve gear, the first example of a type which would become commonplace in Britain. The layout of the frames, cylinders and valve gear followed closely a standard design produced by the North British Locomotive Company for the Indian railways, following the move of that company's Chief Estimator to take up the post of Urie's Chief Draughtsman. The design was completed by a Drummond pattern boiler and superstructure. The first ten engines were built in two batches during 1914 but no more appeared until after the formation of the Southern Railway, when a further ten to a slightly modified design with a straight running plate and a Maunsell taper boiler were built in 1924-25. The remaining six were 'major rebuilds/conversions' from Drummond engines, making a total of twenty-six. Unlike the 'S15' 4-6-0s of which seven survive, none of the 'H15's were preserved.

Short framed 'M7' No. 30248 with the front sandboxes on the splasher and built at Nine Elms in 1897, threads its way over the pointwork with a train of Bulleid-designed coaches. It was allocated to Nine Elms from 1948 until withdrawn in July 1961. The 'M7's were eventually displaced from their long-standing duties by BR 'Standard' tanks, with the last one going in early 1963.

The regular smaller tank engines, the 'M7' 0-4-4Ts and '57XX' 0-6-0PTs at this date, were supplemented by the big 'H16' 4-6-2Ts from Feltham when the latter worked in stock from sidings further away than Clapham. Typically, this happened most frequently on summer Saturdays, although this picture of No. 30519 was taken on a Wednesday, 23rd August 1961.

Great Western Railway '57XX' Class 0-6-0PT No. 4681 arrived at Nine Elms from Danygraig in October 1959, to share ECS workings with the native 'M7's. The lever reverse of the ex-GWR engines was appreciated by the Nine Elms men, although not the cramped cab! Also, their power was liked – their ability to lift a heavy train away without fuss.

Not all of the ECS workings went to Clapham Junction yard, with No. 4692 taking these coaches to Wimbledon on 25th August 1961. The '57XX' was one of the first of the class to arrive on the Southern Region, in January 1959, staying at Nine Elms until July 1963, when it went to Exmouth Junction.

CHAPTER 11 - CLAPHAM JUNCTION

When the Southern Region BR 'Standard' 2-6-4Ts were displaced by diesel and electric traction in the early 1960s, several of them were transferred to Nine Elms during 1964-65 to work the ECS trains. Interestingly, there is no record of No. 80082 ever having been on the shed's books; the last allocation recorded was Eastleigh in June 1962, up to withdrawal in September 1966. The locomotive was originally on the London Midland Region, sent to Bletchley when new in 1954 and transferring to Bricklayers Arms in late 1959. Note the skeletal-like remains of the overall roof on the 'A' signal box following the collapse of one side of the cabin in May 1965.

No. 82018 also seen here on ECS duties, had been at Exmouth Junction since new in 1952 and arrived at Nine Elms after two months at Eastleigh; it was withdrawn in July 1966. The 'Idris soft drinks' advertisement to the left of No. 82018 was common on many platforms at this date. The company was founded in 1873 by Thomas Howell Williams, who was so struck by the beauty of the Idris Mountains in Wales, near where he lived, that he changed his name to Thomas Idris. The company was formed to manufacture mineral and aerated water, and in 1880 started to produce flavoured drinks. In 1987, the Britvic Company bought the Idris brand.

The large 'Standard' tanks started on ECS workings once they had been displaced from their suburban passenger work by modern traction. Three of the 2-6-4Ts, from left to right, No's 80015, 80089 and 80133, stand in front of the carriage cleaning shed in 1966. Unusually, No. 80015 on the left has standard white lamps rather than the usual Southern white discs. The first two engines had been transferred to Nine Elms in late 1965, following No. 80133 which had been there since November 1964, and by April 1966 the depot had nine of the class. A year later, only four duties remained, three ECS and one covering the Kensington Olympia service. No. 80015 had previously worked on the Central section at Tunbridge Wells West and No. 80089 had been at several Central sheds, whereas No. 80133 had enjoyed a more nomadic existence, starting on the former LT&SR line and then moving to South Wales in 1962, before arriving on the Southern Region at Feltham.

Cross London freight

Transfer freight between the Southern Region yards at Norwood Junction and Hither Green was worked over the West London Extension line from Clapham Junction, through Kensington to the Western Region at Old Oak Common and the northern lines at Willesden, Neasden, Brent and Ferme Park.

Ex-LM&SR '4F' 0-6-0 No. 44441 takes a coal train through Clapham Junction, having come from Feltham via the Barnes Loop line on 23rd August 1961. One of the Crewe 1927-built engines, No. 44441 was allocated to Devons Road for most of the 1950s but then went to Mansfield for a year, returning to London at Cricklewood in January 1960. The vertical cylinder in front of the cab is the AWS vacuum reservoir; the timing reservoir, relay box and battery box were inside the cab.

Stanier '8F' 2-8-0 No. 48301 with a Willesden to Feltham freight via the Barnes loop on 23rd August 1961. It has lost its 14A cast Cricklewood shed plate but has a hand-painted substitute; it was allocated there from May 1959 until October 1962.

Southern freight workings in the London area featured many regular transfer freights exchanging goods traffic with the other companies/regions. When the suburban area was electrified in the 1920s and 1930s, these workings had to fit in between tightly scheduled multiple unit services. These, often heavy, freight trains also had to be hauled up (and down) the sharp inclines of flying junctions, frequently starting away from a signal check. Therefore, a reasonably fast and powerful, engine was needed, in terms of both haulage and braking power, and a three-cylinder 2-6-4T with 5ft 6ins driving wheels and a tractive effort of 29,376 lb was designed to meet this requirement. It made use of the tanks and bogies made surplus by the 'K' Class 2-6-4T rebuilding in 1928, together with other standard components such as the same boiler as on the 'N', 'N1' and 'U1' 2-6-0 classes. The first five 'W' Class engines were built at Eastleigh in 1932 and had right-hand drive and gravity sanding arrangements, which were not converted to steam operation until 1959-60. Another ten were built at Ashford in 1935-36 and had left-hand drive and steam sanding from new. The class were based at Hither Green, Norwood Junction and Stewarts Lane for most of their lives. No. 31914 was on its way to the West London Line from the Brighton side of the junction with a transfer freight to the Western Region or London Midland Region on 23rd August 1961. It was allocated to Norwood Junction from November 1960 until November 1962, when it was one of eight of the 2-6-4Ts transferred to Exmouth Junction to replace withdrawn 'Z' Class 0-8-0Ts, which had been used to bank trains up the 1 in 37 incline between Exeter St. David's and Central stations. The 'W's were not a success in their new role as banking engines, given their inferior adhesion weight, and No. 31914 returned to Norwood Junction at the end of 1963, moving then to Feltham in January 1964 when that shed closed to steam. It was the last of the class to be withdrawn, in August 1964.

Clapham Junction saw a variety of diesel power on cross-London freight trains, such as brand new BR Sulzer Type '2' No. D7666, which had arrived off the West London line on 3rd December 1966. It had just entered traffic from Derby Works as part of an order originally given to Beyer, Peacock but their precarious financial position led to the company asking to be released from the final eighteen locomotives. The batch No's D7660-69 were the first delivered in Rail Blue and were allocated to D01 (London (Western) Division) and based at Willesden for Euston ECS duties and inter-regional freight working. No. D7666 was renumbered as No. 25316 in March 1974 and again to No. 25911 in 1985; it was withdrawn in 1986.

Heading for Feltham with a train of empty 16-ton mineral wagons on 3rd December 1966, Sulzer Type '2' No. D5216 passes under Clapham Junction 'A' signal box. The diesel was built at Derby and entered service at Toton in July 1963, moving south to Cricklewood the following month. No. D5216 stayed there, in what subsequently became D14 London (Midland) Division, until June 1968, when it was transferred to the Western Division D01. It was renumbered to No. 25066 in March 1974 and was in traffic until June 1981.

1960s

Until the introduction of the 'S15' 4-6-0s in 1920, the last goods engines built for or by the L&SWR were the thirty Drummond '700' Class 0-6-0s purchased from Dübs & Co. The design shared many standard parts, including the boiler, firebox, cylinders and motion, with the 'M7' 0-4-4Ts and other contemporary classes. They were displaced in Southern Railway days by the advent of the 'S15's, and later the 'Q' 0-6-0s, relegating the class to secondary duties. Built in May 1897 as L&SWR No. 705, No. 30696 was working a Nine Elms-Feltham freight when photographed here in May 1960. It was shedded at Feltham until withdrawn in August 1961.

'L1' 4-4-0 No. 31788 at Clapham Junction in late-1959, with what appears to be ECS for a Southampton Docks Ocean Liner Express. No. 31788 was at Nine Elms from June 1959 until withdrawn in January 1960.

The variety of what appears to be ex-works stock behind 'K' Class 2-6-0 No. 32338 In May 1960 suggests it is probably delivering vehicles from the carriage works at Lancing and, for the Pullman works at Preston Park. The headcode indicates solely 'via Streatham Spur', which would enable it to get from the Up Brighton line without reversal. No. 32338 was built in 1913 and allocated to Brighton from February 1951 until December 1962. The Billinton 'K' Class 'Moguls' were both the first 2-6-0s built by the LB&SCR and also its first engines with Belpaire fireboxes. The seventeen engines were built between 1913 and 1921.

Highly polished 'Schools' 4-4-0 No. 30926 *Repton* hurries through Clapham Junction with the 12.10pm Victoria to Tattenham Corner Royal Train race special on 31st May 1961. The four white discs indicate a Royal Train and No. 30926 was a regular for Royal Train Derby specials in 1961-62. *Repton* carries a 73A Stewarts Lane shed plate having been transferred from Bricklayers Arms in February 1961. Its AWS and speedometer were fitted in October 1960. Happily, the locomotive survived withdrawal and has been at the North York Moors Railway since 1989, after first spending over twenty years in North America, based at Steamtown USA in Vermont.

'King Arthur' No. 30777 *Sir Lamiel*, built by the North British Locomotive Company in June 1925, had worked ECS back from Waterloo to Clapham Junction on 19th August 1961. The 'Scotch Arthurs' had lower, different profile cabs for the more restricted ex-SE&CR loading gauge. The engine had been transferred to Basingstoke in October 1960, having spent most of the previous decade on the Eastern section at Dover. Now preserved in the National Collection, after withdrawal in October 1961, *Sir Lamiel* was first stored at Fratton, then Stratford and finally Ashford. In June 1978, it was adopted by the Humberside Locomotive Preservation Group (HLPG) and moved to their base at Hull Dairycoates shed, where it was restored for main line operation, making its first run in March 1982. No. 30777 has since worked regularly on the national network and is now in the custody of the 5305 Locomotive Association, the successor to the HLPG, and is based on the Great Central Railway at Loughborough.

'Lord Nelson' No. 30864 *Sir Martin Frobisher* is seen on a Brittany Ferry special from Southampton Docks on 23rd August 1961, its last summer in service. AWS had been fitted in October 1959 and it was withdrawn In January 1962.

'Battle of Britain' No. 34052 *Lord Dowding* approaches the brick-built Clapham Junction B signal box on 2nd September 1966. No. 34052 had been rebuilt in 1958 and was allocated to Salisbury from June 1951 until withdrawal in July 1967.

BRC&W Type '3' No. D6560 heads towards Victoria with an Oxted line train on 2nd September 1966. It was renumbered as No. 33042 under TOPS and was withdrawn in 1996, after thirty-five years in traffic. The large advertisement on the left is for *The Blue Max*, a 1966 film starring George Pepparad and Ursula Andress, about a German fighter pilot on the Western Front during the First World War.

The 'Bournemouth Belle' was diagrammed for 'Merchant Navy' haulage almost until the end of Southern steam in 1967. Seen here with the Down train in 1962, No. 35019 *French Line C.G.T.* runs with steam shut off over the 40mph speed restriction. 'C.G.T.' was an abbreviation of Compagnie Générale Transatlantique, the French shipping company established in the late 19th Century and known overseas as the 'French Line'. No. 35019 was rebuilt in 1959, fitted with AWS in October 1959 and a speedometer in February 1961. It was allocated to Nine Elms from new in June 1945 until September 1964, when that shed transferred all of its 'Pacifics' out to other sheds because labour shortages had made it increasingly difficult to maintain engines there.

One of eighteen 'Light Pacifics' rescued from Woodham Brother's scrapyard at Barry, No. 34016 *Bodmin* on a train to Bournemouth West with a six-coach restaurant car set (a '6 dining set D', in the official carriage working notice terminology) at the front in early 1962. The ECS on the left, from the 'Royal Wessex' which had arrived at Waterloo at 10.50am behind an Eastleigh-allocated engine, would suggest that No. 34016's train is the 11.30am from Waterloo. *Bodmin* was rebuilt in 1958 and, after rescue from Barry scrapyard, was restored at the Mid-Hants Railway. It ran on the main line but has not been in use for several years and is currently awaiting overhaul. The engine was allocated to Eastleigh from May 1961 until withdrawn in June 1964. The speedometer and AWS were fitted in August 1960.

The air-smoothed casing is only just keeping the smoke away from the cab of 'Battle of Britain' No. 34073 *249 Squadron* at Clapham Junction in 1962. Like *Bodmin* above, it was withdrawn in June 1964, after sixteen years in traffic.

'West Country' No. 34028 *Eddystone* on an Up Bournemouth express in 1962. Bournemouth-based at the time of this view, it was allocated to Eastleigh from September 1962 until withdrawn in May 1964, one of the earliest rebuilds to be taken out of service. No. 34028 then went to Barry scrapyard and was purchased in 1986 for £6,000, moving to Sellindge in Kent. After a long restoration period, completed in 2003, it worked on the Swanage Railway until 2014 and is now undergoing a 10-year overhaul.

'Merchant Navy' No. 35020 *Bibby Line*, also on a train from Bournemouth in 1962. It was allocated to Nine Elms from new in June 1945 until September 1964, and was rebuilt in 1956. The bogie van at the front of this train is a BR-built General Utility Vehicle ('GUV'), whereas that behind *Eddystone* is a Southern Railway four-wheeled design termed a Parcels & Miscellaneous Van ('PMV').

The BR 'Standard' Class '5' 4-6-0s allocated to Nine Elms and Stewarts Lane in the late 1950s were all given names from withdrawn 'King Arthur' 4-6-0s, although it was some time before they were all applied to the engines. No. 73118, seen on a train to Basingstoke in 1962, was named in February 1960, taking the name previously used on 'King Arthur' No. 30739 *King Leodegrance*. It was allocated to Nine Elms from new in November 1955 until August 1964, when it was transferred to Eastleigh.

'4-COR' No. 3102 passes through Clapham Junction with a service to Waterloo from Alton via Earlsfield. These units were built in 1937 for the electrification to Portsmouth and had gangways at either end for use when running with a second set, as shown here.

CHAPTER 11 - CLAPHAM JUNCTION

BR 'Standard' Class '4' 2-6-4T No. 80019 was allocated to the Central section from new in October 1951 until its final move in June 1965, to Bournemouth. It was shedded at Tunbridge Wells West from October 1956 until it was transferred to Brighton in September 1963, with this picture probably being taken a few months before that date.

After spending its early years in the north of England at Patricroft and then Grimesthorpe, BR 'Standard' Class '5' 4-6-0 No. 73043 moved to the Southern Region at Eastleigh in late 1962. In May 1965, it transferred to Guildford and then finally to Nine Elms in June 1966. Although the headcode indicates Waterloo to Southampton Terminus, or after its closure Eastleigh, the time table showed few passenger trains from Waterloo terminating at/starting from either, so it is more likely working a Basingstoke 'stopper' in this picture taken in late 1965 or 1966.

The second Southern Railway electric locomotive, No. 20002, was built at Ashford as No. CC2 in September 1945. Although designed as mixed traffic engines, their main work was on freight, although they soon became associated with the Victoria-Newhaven boat trains, replacing the Brighton 'Atlantics' on this duty in 1949. No. 20002 was passing through Clapham Junction on one of these boat trains when photographed here circa 1965, after it was fitted with a headcode panel but before its pantograph was removed in 1966. All three of the electrics were transferred to Stewarts Lane from Brighton in March 1959 and stayed until August 1966, when they returned to the South Coast shed. The three locomotives were classified as Class '70' under TOPS, although they never carried a TOPS number; No's 20002/3 were withdrawn in late 1968 and No. 20001 in January 1969. Note the two different architectural styles used by the L&SWR and LB&SCR on the footbridges.

Diesels

In original 1960 condition without a yellow warning panel, BRC&W Type '3' No. D6517 heads through with a parcels train in the mid-1960s. It was one of nineteen of the class fitted for push-pull operation in 1967 and was renumbered under TOPS as No. 33105. It was withdrawn in 1987 after sustaining severe damage following a collision with a fallen tree.

It is perhaps surprising that the Southern Region appeared to fit more snowploughs to its 'Cromptons' than other English Regions fitted to their diesel fleets. No. D6577, also on parcels work, appears to have recently been in works gaining a small yellow warning panel. It became No. 33058 under TOPS in 1974 and was withdrawn in 1991.

BRC&W Type '3' diesel-electric No. D6541 in front of the carriage cleaning shed at Clapham Junction in the mid-1960s. Built in January 1961, it became No. 33023 in 1974 and spent many years during the 1990s in and out of store, before eventual withdrawal in 1997.

Twelve BRC&W Type '3's were built with narrower, 8ft 8ins wide bodies instead of the standard 9ft 3ins, to allow them to be used on the Tonbridge to Hastings line. This apparently involved the Birmingham Company in a large amount of expensive re-design and the locomotives were not delivered until after all the standard ones were in service, even though they had been ordered almost a year before the final batch of these. They were known by enthusiasts as 'Slim Jims', and were recognisable by their smaller front windows and headcode box, but mainly by the way in which the bodysides continued straight up from the frames, whereas on the standard locomotives these were proud of the frame width. Another of the class fitted with a snowplough, No. D6597 is taking the Stewarts Lane breakdown crane and train through Clapham Junction in the mid-1960s. No. D6597 was the last of the class to enter traffic, in May 1962, and became a Class '33/2' under TOPS, renumbered as No. 33212 in 1974; it was withdrawn in 1987. Note the 'BD' in the headcode box; this is confusing – the Central and South East sections used 'BD' to signify an inter-regional working from Willesden to Plumstead via the West London Line, Nunhead and Blackheath, which would not have passed through Clapham Junction, and in this case it probably just signified 'Breakdown'.

'Warship' No. D820 *Grenville* remained in green until June 1967, when it went into Swindon Works for a Classified repair, completed in July, when it emerged in blue with full yellow ends. The 1O88 headcode was for the 14.20 Exeter-Waterloo service, which No. D820 had brought in before running back to Clapham Junction sidings.

The penultimate Swindon built 'Warship' (they were later redesignated as Class '42'), No. D869 *Zest* waits in the carriage sidings in 1966. It ran in the maroon livery shown until the end of 1969, when it received full yellow ends.

Although the Swindon-built Class '42' 'Warships' had been in regular use on Exeter-Waterloo trains since 1964, the North British Class '43' locomotives were rarely in London on the Southern Region. No. D860 *Victorious* was on a special ECS working at Clapham Junction on 27th June 1967. The Class '42's had a virtual monopoly of the Exeter-Waterloo trains in order to simplify maintenance procedures and crew-training; Salisbury drivers were the only ones with Class '43' training and they were very infrequent substitutes, usually only when there was a failure at the London end.

Diesels from all the Regions added to the variety at Clapham Junction, as illustrated by British Thomson Houston Type '1' No. D8230. The 34G Finsbury Park shedplate dates the photograph to late 1967 or early 1968, before it was transferred to Stratford.

A view of the bonnet end of No. D8230 at Clapham Junction. The 800bhp Type '1' British Thomson Houston Bo-Bo diesel electric was built by the Clayton Equipment Co. at Derby, entering service in July 1960 and originally allocated to Norwich, then briefly to March and next on to Stratford in November 1960, before moving to Finsbury Park in April 1963. Its next move was to Stratford in April 1968 until March 1970, when it had a short spell at Finsbury Park before going back to Stratford. The class was deemed non-standard under the British Railways 1968 Traction Plan and No. D8230 was among the final twenty-three locomotives in the class to remain in service, which were all withdrawn in March 1971.

CHAPTER 11 - CLAPHAM JUNCTION

The diesel-electric shunters on the Southern Region were not used on ECS duties to and from Waterloo because they were limited to a maximum speed of 20mph and thus only appeared at Clapham Junction to shunt the carriage sidings, as illustrated by No. D3465 in June 1958. It was a standard 350hp shunter, built in July 1957 at Darlington and allocated to Hither Green for three months before transfer to Norwood Junction. No. D3465 returned to the former shed in April 1962, became No. 08380 in 1973 under TOPS and was withdrawn in 1982. Note the small 'D' prefix in front of the stock number, and the absence of yellow and black diagonal warning stripes.

Built at Horwich in 1961, No. D4104 was one of the 0-6-0 diesel shunters with 4ft 6ins diameter wheels and gearing to allow a top speed of 27$^{1}/_{2}$ mph, which were built for shunting and branch line freight work on the Southern Region; they became Class '09' under TOPS. No. D4104, pictured at Clapham Junction in 1966, was transferred from Norwood Junction to Feltham in July 1968 and was renumbered as No. 09016 in 1973. Note the high level pipes fitted to all of the Class '09's and some of the Southern Region allocated '08's, in order to shunt primarily EMU stock. No. D4104 is in blue livery with the British Rail double arrow, but its stock number is in the pre-Rail Alphabet characters. The large building in the centre of the picture, resembling a signal box was actually the Yard Foreman's office and shunters' cabin, the latter being on the first floor. It was always busy, with shunters constantly entering and leaving, together with train crews asking for information.

No. D3274 shows off the final version of the blue livery with the British Rail standard Rail Alphabet serif numbers. It still has a 'D' prefix, howeverm which suggests the picture was taken in the late 1960s. Built at Derby in 1956 as No. 13274, it became No. D3274 in September 1959 and gained its third number under TOPS as No. 08204 in 1974. It was at Feltham from the end of 1962 until June 1969, when it went to Eastleigh, and was withdrawn in August 1983. Details to note are the shunter's pole placed carefully across the front bufferbeam, with one end above the buffer and the other below, and the Southern style white disc above the left-hand buffer.

Electro-Diesels

The six prototype 'JA' electro-diesels were immediately successful, with a further thirty being ordered in June 1963 and, soon after, thirteen more were authorised; all were in service by January 1967. Classified 'JB', they were distinguishable from the 'JA's since they had one less high level multiple unit jumper cable and one less body side window. They also had different traction motors, allowing a top speed of 90mph, 10mph higher than the 'JA's. This is the first of the 'JB' production series, No. E6007, which was delivered in October 1965 from English Electric's Vulcan Foundry in Lancashire, in rail blue with light grey band and no ownership markings; the grey band, which was only used on the first seven locomotives, really set the livery scheme off. No. E6007 was renumbered No. 73101 in 1974 but temporarily became No. 73100 in December 1980 as part of the centenary celebrations of the local Brighton newspaper, when it was also named *Brighton Evening Argus*. It reverted to No. 73101 after three weeks but kept the nameplates until April 1982. Ten years later, it was again given a temporary name, *The Royal Alex*, as part of an appeal on behalf of the Brighton Children's Hospital, the plates remaining in place until 1996. The locomotive was withdrawn in 2004.

The later 'JB' electro-diesels had a plain blue body with the British Rail double arrow positioned centrally, though still with a small yellow warning panel. No. E6037 was delivered from Vulcan Foundry in July 1966, became No. 73130 in 1974 and carried the name *City of Portsmouth* between 1988 and 1993. Along with No. 73118, it was taken over by Eurostar and fitted with Scharfenburg couplings to enable it to tow the Eurostar sets when they had failed or over non-electrified lines, being used in that role until 2007.

Built in January 1966, No. E6016 became No. 73110 in 1974 and worked until 2002. It was preserved and is now at the Great Central Railway in Nottingham. On the right, parked on the siding next to Platform 6 which, with the one next to it, extended almost to Wandsworth Town, is an uncommon visitor to London, DEMU No. 1116, one of the 1959-built, two-car 'Hampshire' units, most of which were augmented by a Second Class centre gangway trailer, as in this case. Again it carries a black inverted triangle on this end, signifying the end of the unit containing the luggage compartment, to assist station staff who had parcels to load or collect.

CHAPTER 11 - CLAPHAM JUNCTION

When the Bournemouth electrification was completed in 1967, a need was identified for a locomotive capable of hauling the heavy boat train services to Southampton, which involved working over non-electrified lines in the dock area. Ideally, the requirement for ten locomotives would have been met by using pairs of Class '73' electro-diesels but twenty of these could not be made available. At the same time, the amount of freight traffic on the Southern Region had declined and some of the Class '71' electrics had become surplus to requirements. A plan to convert them to dual-power operation was put together in conjunction with English Electric, the main sub-contractor. Diesel power was to be provided by a Paxman Ventura 650hp diesel engine, coupled to an English Electric generator, chosen because it was a small, light, fast running unit and was already in use in the Western Region Class '14' 0-6-0 diesel-hydraulics. The conversion significantly increased the weight and the body structure had to be considerably strengthened to become load-bearing, which was done by putting in a girder framework. The original 2,500hp booster set and four traction motors were retained and to operate the locomotives, advanced solid state electronic control equipment was installed. They were also modified to work in multiple with each other, as well as Class '73's, Class '33's and EMUs. The ten Class '71's in the poorest condition were selected for conversion and the work was carried out at Crewe. It was a protracted affair, with the first converted locomotive, No. E6101, finally delivered in November 1967, after thirteen months, and the tenth, No. E6110, in June 1968. As soon as they entered traffic, serious problems emerged with the electronic control equipment and in addition to these, numerous minor technical issues arose. There was a dramatic decline in the boat train traffic in the early 1970s and the Class '74's were increasingly used on freight duties but their continuing unreliability saw them earmarked for withdrawal in 1976. No. E6104, standing in front of the carriage shed at Clapham Junction, was the original No. E5000, which had been renumbered to No. E5024 in December 1962. It was taken out of service for conversion to an electro-diesel in October 1966, although no work appears to have been done on it for almost a year but was eventually completed in February 1968, becoming No. E6104. It was fitted with a prototype Automatic Warning System which, for the first time, displayed actual signal aspects in the cab and was the forerunner of future AWS and cab warning systems. It was renumbered as No. 74004 in December 1973 and was withdrawn at the end of 1977, along with the other seven Class '74's then remaining in service.

EMUs in the 1960s and 1970s

The '4-CIG' was the first of a new generation of express multiple units which were based on the '4-CEP' units built for the Kent Coast electrification. A major difference was the decision to house the traction and control equipment, previously carried on the driving vehicles, in an intermediate Motor Brake Second. The front-end appearance was tidied-up, with rounded edges to the driving ends and the jumper cables enclosed in a recess. Thirty-six '4-CIG' sets and eighteen of the corresponding '4-BIG' Buffet car sets were ordered from York in 1962, to replace the pre-war Pullman and Pantry car sets on the Central section. Another 102 '4-CIG' and ten '4-BIG' sets were subsequently introduced for the Waterloo-Portsmouth services and, more generally, to replace Southern Railway-design stock on both the South Western and Central divisions. The first units were finished in the standard plain green livery with small yellow warning panels, as shown by No. 7313 on a Victoria-Brighton non-stop. The initial batch of '4-CIG/BIG's ran only on the 'Brighton', although they did reach Portsmouth from Victoria via the Mid-Sussex line. They differed from the later batch, running on Mk4 rather than Mk6 motor bogies and were fitted with an electric parking brake. The interior was very similar to the '4CEP/BEP's as built; the later batches were rather more austere.

Newly delivered from British Rail Engineering Ltd at York, No. 7720 was the last of the first batch of twenty '4-VEP's (four-coach Vestibule Electro-Pneumatic) built in 1967 for semi-fast services. The front-end design followed that of the '4-BIG' units, with rounded edges to the driving ends and jumper cables enclosed in a recess, Pullman type gangways and buck-eye couplers but, in essence, they were little different from their immediate predecessors, with slam doors to every seating row; in fact, they were the last stock built in this configuration. A total of 194 sets entered service between 1967 and 1974, and they eventually accounted for around seventy-five per cent of outer suburban duties. They became Class '423' under TOPS.

In 1967, the newly electrified Bournemouth line services were formed with a '4-REP' Motor Buffet set at the London end, as illustrated by No. 3001, and occasionally in the middle, together with one or two '4-TC' trailer sets. After detaching from the '4-REP' at Bournemouth, these were powered by a push-pull fitted Class '33/1' diesel over the non-electrified section to Weymouth. In appearance, the front end was almost identical to the '4-CIG' and '4-VEP', and the passenger accomodation was essentially the BR Mark 1, with the two trailer vehicles rebuilt in true Southern fashion from former loco-hauled Mark 1s. Eleven '4-REP's were built and they were delivered in the uninspiring plain rail blue livery shown on No. 3001, although they were subsequently repainted in the express passenger blue/grey livery. A further four sets were built in 1974, to enable the Bournemouth/Weymouth fast service frequency to be increased from two-hourly to hourly.

Left: An indication that we are now in the 1970s, 'MIND THE GAP' has been painted on the platform edges. '4-EPB' No. 5370 waiting at Platform 13, was built in 1963 with a body profile which was the same as the standard BR compartment stock.

Right: '2-EPB' No. 5752 forms the front half of a Chessington South service which has just arrived at Plaform 10. These were a two-car version of the '4-EPB', introduced in 1954 to enable the standard suburban multiple unit train formation to be increased from eight to ten cars.

Below: '4-VEP' No. 7723 from the second batch built in 1968, on a Waterloo-Bournemouth stopping service.

CHAPTER 11 - CLAPHAM JUNCTION

Left: The 'Brighton Belle' was one of the regular daily attractions for observers at Clapham Junction in the early 1970s. When introduced in 1933 as the 'Southern Belle', it was the first all-electric Pullman train in the world. There were three return trips each day, originally running non-stop in a time of sixty minutes. The three five-car '5-BEL' sets received their final overhauls, during which their Pullman burnt umber and cream was replaced by BR blue and grey, between December 1968 and May 1969, and the final run of the 'The Belle' was on Sunday 30th April 1972. Six of the vehicles have been preserved by the '5-BEL' Trust and are currently being restored with the aim of returning the train to the main line in the next few years. It will run as a '6-BEL' including an extra car fitted with a larger kitchen for enhanced catering.

Right: An unusual view with four trains in picture. Nearest the camera is '4-VEP' No. 7813 on a Waterloo-Basingstoke service. It was built in 1970 and was delivered in the blue and grey livery which replaced the overall blue on all of these units in the early 1970s.

Below: Another '4-VEP', No. 7749, in the sidings at Clapham Junction in the early 1970s.

The young spotter has just had time to record the 'Crompton' on the left as '4-VEP' No. 7816 speeds towards him on a Portsmouth & Southsea Low Level stopping service. The Class '33' is No. 6552, which was taking a train of Presflo cement wagons down towards the West London line.

In 1970, British Rail decided to build a prototype new generation electric multiple unit to try out the changes required going forward, since many of the older types were becoming due for replacement. Two four-car sets and one two-car set were ordered for testing on the Southern Region, being classified as 'PEP' (Prototype Electro Pneumatic). The units had sliding doors, low-backed seating, electric rheostatic braking in addition to the standard electro-pneumatic, and all vehicles were to be powered to provide the required acceleration capability. After extensive testing, the units went into public service out of Waterloo in June 1973 and almost immediately were greeted with howls of protest from the travelling public, who disliked the hard, short-backed seats and the fact that many of them were forced to stand because the number of seats was reduced by over twenty-five per cent from their existing trains. No. 4001 is seen here coupled with the other four-car set, No. 4002, on a Shepperton to Waterloo via Wimbledon service. Note the fourth vehicle in the train is in unpainted aluminium; this was one of the coaches from the '2-PEP' unit which had replaced one of the blue DBMS coaches in No. 4001 in late 1972. The units worked on the South Western section, based at Wimbledon, until October 1976. Although short-lived, they achieved their purpose and paved the way for the new designs which came into service at the end of the decade. The Class '508' units introduced in 1979 looked similar in appearance and were one of several classes derived from the prototypes. They were intended for the Liverpool area but stock shortages on the Southern saw them diverted there until delivery of the Class '455' units allowed them to move to the Merseyrail area.